"My friend Daniel Lusko is a director in Hollywood, and his life is proof his imagination is well exercised. Daniel's book does an excellent job of showing us how to fire up our imagination and channel its magnificent creative power toward the good we desire. This book should be kept on hand and reviewed again and again. It is absolutely power-packed with unfailing principles and experiences of the imagination that will ignite your mind and change your life!"

-BOB PROCTOR

New York Times Bestselling Author
Leading Contributor of "The Secret"
Founder of The Proctor Gallagher Institute

IMAGINATION
CREATES REALITY

*How to awaken your imagination
and realize your dreams.*

DANIEL LUSKO

Published by Daniel Lusko

Cover Design & Book Layout: Kent Locke

First Edition Printed: 2018

ISBN: 9781976932700

"If one advances confidently in the direction of his dreams, and endeavors to live the life which he has imagined, he will meet with a success unexpected in common hours."

-Henry David Thoreau

CONTENTS

INTRODUCTION

The power of the imagination is a phrase often relevant to only a select few who are considered creative people. Why are some people creative and others are not? Is the imagination something that is available only to inventors and artists? There is so much more to the imagination that is relevant to every single person on the planet, and whether consciously or unconsciously, something that each one of us are influenced by every single moment of our lives. With this book, my aim is to expand the awareness and skill of the reader's extraordinary power to use their imagination to create the life of their dreams that all of mankind will benefit from.

Through this book, I intend to prove that each and every person has access to the very same power as the greatest people in history. Plenty of books out there explain the law of attraction, but I've found none in all my searching that clearly reveals the synthesis of awareness between the use of faith and imagination that is accessible to anyone of any age. Children in schools spend a significant portion of their lives learning curriculums full of information they will never remember and never use. Teachers overemphasize teaching memorization, instead of nurturing a child's imagination. They put very little if any time teaching children to develop their own mind, while they obsess over knowledge designed by the opinions of unimaginative people. Kids wander around school campuses for decades piling up a fortune of debt only to exit with a useless degree and crippled by a lack of purpose. Schools and churches ought to make the imagination the first subject children learn and empower them to think for themselves. They should know the greatest men in history are not of the academic kind, but men who dared to dream for themselves a better world. I wrote this book as straightforward as possible, so that the educated and uneducated could read it and decide for themselves what they think. It is my desire this knowledge would multiply itself and make its way into every school on the planet, so that we would raise up a generation of children not dependent on a system they cannot rely on, but instead to rely on their own imagination to make the world a better place for everyone.

I've watched devout religious people cringe at the word "imagination," when it is used outside of the arts. They conjure in their minds vague ideas of idolatry like Aladdin rubbing his lamp to create selfish manifestations for his greedy purposes. Besides religious groups, you have so-called immoral creative types broadly touting the power of their imagination and the work they create, while shrinking over the word "faith," in fear it might summon the power of God from high above to strike them with a lightning bolt for their sins. Both extremes are ignorant of the one power to will and to do flowing to and through all mankind. The imaginative liberal artist working in Hollywood and the devout religious monk walking by faith are both working with the same exact power.

The power of imagination is not given to a select few, but it is properly used by a select few. If you're not aware of how to use your imagination, it can be the hardest work in the world to create the life of your dreams. This is because your imagination is attached to your circumstances, and it's replaying what you've been experiencing over and over like a record. You can try to change your life, but inevitably it will revert back unless you have the awareness and skill to overcome the paradigm that is locked in your subsconscious mind. Dysfunctional paradigms are why many people remain stuck in dead end jobs, and fail to ever accomplish anything of value.

This virus is the norm among society, which is why people feel comfortable remaining this way. It's also why people are shocked and amazed when someone breaks their paradigm and makes a difference in this world. Anyone who gives their attention to the coming pages in a meaningful way will have that same power.

Did you know you have beliefs which were inherited from people in your family lineage you have never met? Those behavior patterns have controlled your life without you even knowing it. Your paradigm is about to change, and by the end of this book, you will know you have what it takes. Most people will never even consider this reality or try to change it. They are walking zombies, reacting automatically to the world with beliefs inherited from their ancestors. They will never stop to ask themselves what do they believe and what do they want their life to be like? You are not your name. You are not your body. You inherited these things. You determine your beliefs. You determine your reality. You determine the life you create.

The imagination can be used for evil just like it can be used to create the most wonderful things in the world. There are specific techniques to bring about what some would call miracles in important areas of your life. In this book, I will help you develop a clear understanding of how to master your thought life in a way that brings your dreams in perfect harmony with your reality.

We all have paradigms in our subconscious, and many of those beliefs have been in there from well-before we were able to discern for ourselves what we believed. If you come from a religious or anti-religious background, you may have an aversion to the word "faith," or "imagination," depending on which background you come from. You may not believe you have the power to create, to heal, to lead, or to change. There is much more between the lines of these pages than the simple words printed on them.

This book speaks with simple language, but within these seemingly simple stories and ideas is the power to not only transform your life into the one you've dreamed of, but also to transform the lives of every single person around you. What gives me the right to make such a claim? Because of my own personal experiences outlined in this book, and those who have read these pages with an open mind and their personal experiences. Your own personal experiences will tell you the same. Every single person in the world today has the same creative energy flowing through them as the greatest leaders in history. The greatest problem is unbelief. People are looking to something outside themselves to solve their problems. The power of God is within each person, and their life is dictated by what they think. As you open your mind and heart to the truth, I trust you will find in these pages the answers you've been looking for.

As you read, I ask that you take your time moving through it. It's not intended to be read in a rush. When you come upon an idea that makes you think, do just that. Stop and think about it. Allow these truths to sink in, and they can change your life. To benefit from the truth written in this book, you must at all times cast aside the doubts placed in your mind by the opinions of others, and begin at once to think and decide for yourself what you believe.

1. POWER OF AWARENESS

"Your only limitations are those you set up in your own mind, or permit others to set up for you."

O.G. Mandino

As I was preparing for a film I would soon direct about a CIA operative, I decided to put myself in the shoes of the character; I underwent immersive CIA training with a former Chief of Country for a special unit in the CIA. Over the course of months training with a "real Jason Bourne," I learned the importance of situational awareness. Of those who apply for the CIA, only about 1% actually make it past the pre-qualifying testing period. And of those who make through that rigorous process, a majority end up working desk jobs - only a small percentage actually make it to the field in the operational community. Suffice it to say, it is a small club. The CIA is looking for a distinct quality in their people, something beyond just intelligence.

Operatives must be able to remain calm and focused under extreme pressure, even in life threatening situations. This quality is what makes it possible for them to accomplish the mission, whatever that might be. This acute situational awareness the CIA is looking for is something proposed by Malcom Gladwell in his book, "Blink." Gladwell believes that this trait can be taught, so that you are able to respond spontaneously in a way that is fruitful in any situation. People with this quality are those who may hear an alarm go off, and rather than panic, they become calm and focused. They know automatically what to do to accomplish their pre-determined mission.

The months of training I spent with these extraordinary men reminded me of a lesson that is relevant to all of us. It is something that is so rarely spoken of or talked about, but is so important to living the life of your dreams and getting the results you want. It's the power of attention. On the surface it seems so simple. People talk about their goals. They have a desire to live a happy life. They want to be joyful. They have desires. But, at the first sign of trouble or obstacles, they switch gears to something else and are constantly focusing on whatever comes in their way - rather than those goals they set forth to achieve. He or she who debates between doing one of two things will do neither!

It's remarkable to me that in the most elite circles of entertainment, politics or religion, how few people seem to grasp the importance of awareness. Most people are focused on what they don't want and they wonder why their circumstances are uncongenial. Perhaps it makes them feel better for a time to relish in the negativity. People seem to have no trouble understanding the point when it comes to a person who commits a horrible crime. They learn how that person spent their days constantly meditating on the things they hate until finally they couldn't take it any longer and they shoot up a mall or a movie theater. At the same rate, you have extraordinary power within your awareness to create wonderful things that bring you joy and bring joy to others. This power is not limited to a select group of people; this is a gift that your Creator has given to everyone. And yet it is something that few people understand. Every single one of us carries an inner-conversation that we take with us throughout the day. Take a moment and listen to the conversations that you hear at work, at school, at the coffee shop, setting aside any reservations you might have of whether you agree with such points. Just listen to what is being said. A majority of what is being said is negative! And, what's more, people will justify it all day long, arguing that they need to spread the word or they need to tell the truth.

There are assumptions that people make which reach into every part of who they are. What you recognize in someone else, you recognize in yourself because we are all part of the whole as children of our Creator. Or, to look at it another way, we are all made up of energy, which means we are all connected at that level. When you transmit negative energy, you are emitting a certain frequency not just about that subject, but you are also sending messages into your body through your central nervous system into every part of your being and into the world around you. How do you get on a different frequency?

"Be still and know that I am God."

Psalms 46:10

Your "I" is your consciousness of being. For instance, when you are excited you say "I am joyful," or when you find yourself ill you say, "I am sick." You are designating "I am," somewhere every moment of every day. You are determining what state you want to see more of. You are making a declaration that will externalize itself in your world. Most people do this carelessly. They never give this any thought, completely unaware of the repercussions. They spend their lives reacting to conditions. You have the power to decide where you place your "I" of attention. That seems simple. In fact, too simple for the wisdom of the world to understand, so people write it off as new age "prosperity thinking," and go back to complaining. Your conditions are the result of your thinking, and your thoughts and feelings consist of limitless power with which you have been entrusted! People are constantly putting their stock in something outside of themselves to bring them joy. When those circumstances change or disappoint them, they fall in consciousness and the cycle repeats itself over and over again. They look for satisfaction in a person, a bank account balance, or a circumstance. But that is not where joy is found. There are wonderful experiences to be enjoyed, but they are not the source; they are the out-picturing of an internal state. When someone gives you a wonderful gift on your birthday, it's because they love you. The source is not the gift, it's the thoughts and feelings in the relationship that produced the gift. It's wonderful to enjoy the gift to the extent that you recognize and appreciate the source. The key is to completely stop looking for validation from without and recognize that you have the power of thought. If any of your circumstances are unfavorable, there is nobody to blame except yourself. One way to check to see how well you manage your attention is to sit in a room for twenty minutes, remain completely still, and let go of your thoughts completely to see where they go. You will realize how little control you actually exercise in your attention and how much your attention drifts from subject to subject. Try it!

"The wind is never for the sailor who knows not what port he is bound."

O.G. Mandino

Until we recognize this simple truth, we are constantly building up with one hand and tearing down with the other. We self-sabotage our hopes and dreams, because we build up that idea, while at the same time tearing down someone or something; complaining hurts the other person or thing as much as it hurts ourselves. Many of us would say that we are loving people. Maybe we try not to complain much, but inside we still have conversations going on which are not loving or positive at all. This is where the real work is done. We have the power to bring light into those dark areas of our mind by changing our inner-conversations, first thing in the morning, throughout the day, and before we go to sleep. We must lift up our thoughts! You can't just wait to see what comes up and then decide what to do with it. If you go throughout life with no well-defined idea of what you want, no accidental force outside is going to walk into your life and bring you joy simply because you're such a great person.

You might be thinking that you are so beautiful that a director is going to walk up to you and say, "You're star material! I'm going to make you famous!" I'm a Hollywood director and I deal with famous people often, both behind and in front of the camera. It doesn't work that way. The measure of the effort within is the power that shapes the circumstances. There may be qualities you see in the lives of successful people that make you wonder how they achieved success when they appear to be degenerates or destructive. However, those qualities are not the cause of the success you see. Those conditions are the result of long-sustained thought. A man can rise by lifting up his thoughts, and then easily fall once success is guaranteed, descending to the pavement for all to see. Joy in your thought life and therefore in harmonious circumstances can only be preserved by watchfulness.

"One of the great pitfalls in attempting to use the law of assumption is to focus your attention on things."

Neville Goddard

Recognize where your attention is and learn the art of taking every thought captive. To become aware of what thoughts you are allowing to take root in your mind is so simple and yet so massive that it almost seems impossible. I am here to tell you that it is possible! It is in our thoughts that seeds are planted - and they take root in our soul, which some refer to the subconscious, and through the mysterious power of our Creator make their way into our circumstances and relationships automatically. I cannot tell you when or how they will, for those ways are beyond finding out. However, it is clear that we must be aware of our thoughts, lifting them up so that we find our circum-stances coming into perfect harmony. You will begin to recognize patterns in your daily life. If you stub your toe getting out of bed in the morning, and then curse over it, your day will quickly snowball into a bad one. I heard a bank teller once say, "I had a bad morning, and I just can't shake it." I wanted to reach over the counter and look her in the eyes and say, "Yes you can. It's as simple as believing you can!" The time between believing it and seeing the results is when most people struggle. Because they are so fixated on their conditions they don't see proof, so they return to old ways. The joy that transcends circumstances is something that goes beyond waiting for proof. It's a confidence of faith, one where you are not seeking proof in your conditions.

> ## *"Seek first the kingdom of God and all these things shall be added unto you."*
>
> ### *Jesus*

When we allow seeds of hate to take root under any justification, that too multiplies and comes back to hit us through unexpected means. When you begin to make choices in your inner conversations, you will begin to notice that you have an amazing power to bring that joy into every relationship and circumstance that you encounter. People look at others who are positive and they wonder what makes them so happy. They must have some magnetism that don't. Right? Wrong. It is not the particles that make something magnetic; it is the arrangement of those particles. It is the same with our thoughts. It's the arrangement of your thoughts that your feelings follow and that harmony is where joy is formed. Lift up your thoughts! When someone gets sick they often spend their time telling everyone how sick they are. Every single thought that you have sends a ripple through the cosmos and it comes back multiplied. This is a power that our Creator has given us. How are you using your thoughts? Wouldn't it be amazing for you to begin to use your thoughts to bring joy into this world? What often happens is people try this for a little while, and when they don't see the results they hope for, they return to their old ways of thinking. This key to joy is all about first recognizing what you're giving your attention to, so that you're ready to plant seeds that will grow into trees of magnificent proportions. You have the power of awareness within you. What are you doing with it? Every single moment is an opportunity to invest those thoughts. The exciting part is once you recognize where your "I" of attention is throughout the day, you will find that you desire to bring light into those areas.

Try this simple exercise. Sit for twenty minutes alone in a comfortable chair, but do not lounge. Now let all of your thoughts go and simply be still. When your mind begins to wander and analyze, as it most surely will, ask yourself, where is my "I" of attention. If you have difficulty remaining still, concentrate on your breathing. Take a deep breath in, hold it, and then slowly breathe out. As you do this, your ego will tell you that this is all just a waste of time and to forget it. But as long as you give into that voice that says you have to seek your joy from something on the outside, you are still a slave to conditions, and you will continue in that unending circle. Set a timer if it helps you, but do not look at it or allow it to distract you. One thing that helps me is to close my eyes, or pick an exact mark on the wall and focus on it for the entire time. You will find that once you get in the "zone," it will become effortless to concentrate.

Once you have mastered the skill of remaining still and letting go of your thoughts, try simply concentrating on the words "I Am." This will help cast out distractions and bring you back to the recognition that you have the power of thought and you don't need the distractions that are trying to pull at you. And when your attention drifts, bring it back as many times as it takes until it becomes habit to remain still. Make a habit of taking 20 minutes to do this every day, and it will pay you dividends throughout your life.

For those who love to get things done as I do, you will find that once you learn to "be still," you will be able to do them effortlessly. Hunches will come to you that will remove the strain from rigorous activity, and you will find joy in activities that previously seemed unpleasant. It is in this quiet place that you will experience a freedom that you have never known before. So many people have the impression that to speak with your Creator you must use a certain magic word, or rub a lamp for that matter, but the reality is the energy that formed your being is often heard most clearly in the silence. This quiet place is where you will face where you have been investing your thoughts. You may want to journal the results because by the end of this journey you will be amazed at how your thought life has changed! If you have fear or worry or hatred in your mind, you will confront it here. It is in this place you will see that you can blame nobody else for your thoughts, feelings, or circumstances.

Once you have done this, you will be enthusiastic about proceeding to the next key where we will learn how to use the power of awareness to bring unending joy to your life and those around you.

2. MAGIC OF GRATITUDE

"We should certainly count our bless-ings, but we should also make our blessings count."

Neal A. Maxwell

We are bound to experience adversity and discouragement in the world around us. It's everywhere we look. Often we don't even have to step out of bed. We might wake up from a bad dream or reach over to our phone to see news of something horrific that has happened in another country. All of that influences us. We have a choice in that moment, and few seem to realize the gravity of it. We can change the world by making a decision within ourselves to find something to be grateful for instead of wallowing in negativity. Do you want to live a joyful life, or do you want to live an endless life of complaint? You might say you don't have a choice and that everything around you is awful. As such, you can pick any number of things to concentrate your attention on to prove that this belief is true. And guess what? It will be true and you will align evidence to suggest that. You will share it with those around you, and you will attract people who will validate it; it will perpetuate and it will grow. What you focus on grows. You know from the previous chapter you have the power to direct your attention. And you also can see really how few of us make decisions with our attention moment to moment. Now it's time to change that. We all really have so much to be grateful for, but we tend to overlook it.

"Every day I remind myself that my inner and outer life are based on the labors of other men, living and dead, and that I must exert myself in order to give in the same measure as I have received and am still receiving."

Albert Einstein

It has been said that gratitude is the highest form of love. Gratitude is a state of being. It's not a matter of just giving lip service by saying thank you to the waiter who served you or the person who opened the door. In fact, it really isn't a matter of saying something. It happens internally when you feel joy for something, and it could be the smallest thing in the world. Think of the person stranded in the desert with no water who stumbles upon a pond and fresh fruit. They may in fact feel more gratitude than the billionaire who receives a check for millions of dollars, but it's simply a matter of perspective. You have a choice.

Start with the small things in your life. Do you have clean running water? There are countless people in the world who do not. Do you have groceries? Think of how many people it took to transport that sandwich or cup of coffee so that it could make it into your hands. Do you have clothes on your back? Every time I go into my closet and look at my clothes, I marvel at how much I have and say thank you to all of the people it took to stitch those clothes and transport them. Imagine the faces of the millions of people who do not have even one shirt to call their own. And what about electricity? When I flip a light switch on, I like to imagine what the faces would look like of the billions of people who lived on this earth without electricity. Can you imagine how excited they would be? Billions of people would marvel and yet we do it without the slightest appreciation for what it took for that invention to make its way into our house or office. Every time I switch on a light I get filled with joy, and I give thanks for Thomas Edison for persisting long enough to make this invention a reality. Smartphones are another great reason to be thankful. I've heard so many people complain about how they paid for this new phone and how it only has 16GB of memory on it. Are you kidding me? Thank you, Steve Jobs! I remember when I was in high school and flip phones were just coming out. I was so excited that I would be able to put my friends' names into my phone. Can you imagine how excited and grateful you would have been to tell yourself that in the not too distant future you would have a phone that you could run your entire business from, watch movies, store libraries of music, and interact with the entire world through social media? It all really starts with awareness. Once you recognize what you have and give thanks for it, it's impossible to feel anything but gratitude for all that we have.

How can we not be grateful for what we have? By just being grateful, it makes us more appreciative for what we have, it inspires others to appreciate what they have, and it makes us aware of just how blessed we are. And then we are driven to be more generous with others! When we take what we have for granted and think we're entitled to these privileges because they are common, we start thinking of ourselves instead of others. We ask, "Why don't I have more? That person has so much! What about me?" This is a mentality of lack, and it's a trap which repeats itself, sending messages to your body and brain that you don't have enough. We have cells in our body which are like little workmen carrying out orders all over. When we give these workmen messages that we don't have enough, they repeat that message all over our body. Can you imagine those little workmen making their way down your central nervous system after they met with the boss up in your mind who just told them, "Hey guys, we really didn't do well last quarter, so we're gonna be tightening up around here. There might be cutbacks, maybe even some downsizing. We're in a total state of lack." Then those millions of little workers go marching like worker ants throughout your body repeating that message all day long. What happens? Your body starts tightening up. You feel stiff and disjointed. You look for things that prove to yourself that you're in a state of lack. You see a bank and you clench up. You see a piece of mail come in and you become nervous, because you assume that it's just another bill from someone who wants to take more of what you don't have. You see where this leads. You are the boss, so what orders are you sending throughout your body and mind?

Why not start changing those messages that you're sending to yourself and to everyone around you? This where gratitude becomes key! Instead of your boss focusing on what is lacking, he talked about how much he appreciated everyone for their work? Those men would go back to work energized and excited to do better and create more. The wonderful thing is that when you do that, you're not just sending messages in your body, you're sending messages of gratitude to everyone in the world.

We're all made up of energy. Energy can neither be created nor destroyed, and every cause must have an effect. Every single thought is a cause. The good news is gratitude, which is just another form of love, is much more powerful than negativity. Try it. Watch what happens when you're in a negative conversation with someone who is endlessly complaining, and you point out something you're grateful for at a break in the conversation. It sends a ripple effect through the conversation that you will both feel. They may go back to something negative because they are on that track, but it will only take a few positive comments to change the course of a negative conversation. People will often look at you a little surprised, but don't let that throw you off and send you back into the pool of complaining. When you give into that, you drag yourself down with them. You can lift them up, too! I'm not saying to hit them over the head or put it in their face. That's not gratitude. What I'm saying is to genuinely find a way to change the tone of the conversation in a kind way. One thing that does not work is repeating back to them how negative they are, because it just brings more attention to the negativity and causes that to grow. What you focus on grows! Things will go wrong throughout your day, your week, and your year. There's going to be things that sneak up on you. That's why practicing gratitude before the storm hits is so important. Reactions in those situations are automatic. You respond based upon what you've been thinking about and feeling in all that time leading up to that moment. That's why it's crucial to give thanks for the small things and the big things every second of every day, because when you do, you can turn that moment of adversity into a moment of gratitude. This is where your inner world and your outer world can come into harmony. We should be investing each moment in love, and one way you can always do that is through gratitude. Give thanks that you have eyes to read this book right now! Feel that gratitude and let it permeate your being and reach down into your heart.

Many scientists theorize that your heart actually is a more powerful center of energy than your brain. When I give thanks, I imagine that joy reaching down into my heart as I take a breath in. Then, as I breathe out, I feel love flowing from my chest, up my neck and out my mouth into the world. This cycle can be repeated every moment of every day, and when you are aware of it, it has an effect on every conversation you enter, even those you may have been dreading previously. You will have strength to be positive where previously you may have been overcome with negativity. This is the beginning of changing your inner-conversations, and it is such a simple way to do it! You don't need some clever words or some intellectual or theological magic. We all have the power to be grateful, because we all have breath in our lungs.

Every morning when I wake up, whether I feel groggy or not, I make it a point to give thanks to my Creator for the life that I have. We've been given another day when others have not! This is vital. Don't rush out of bed. What good can you possibly be if you're walking into a situation feeling frustrated or coming from a place of lack? Throughout my day I look for anything and everything to be grateful for. If I run into a prob-lem where perhaps I receive an unexpected bill or a complaint, or anything that might lead me to a place

of complaint, I take a breath and say to myself,
"Thank you God for the perfect outcome with this situation." I will tell you more often than not something
will happen in that moment that will change the outcome. If that outcome persists and leads me to other
reasons to complain, I will fight darkness with light
and continue to look in my mind for something to be
grateful for in that situation.

I received a letter from the IRS about a company of
mine being fined for late filing on taxes. My accountant believed that they had been filed on time. I looked
at our records, and it showed that we had indeed filed
on time. The fine was more money than myself or the
company had at the time. Rather than complaining
about the IRS, I remembered all of the people who
work at the IRS who have families they have to sup-
port. I thought of the kids they have at home and the
mouths to feed. I gave thanks for those people because they help collect money that pays for our high-
ways which allow us to get places fast and our amazing military that puts their lives on the line to keep us
safe while we enjoy our lives. Before you know it my
attitude was changed. I spoke with my accountant
only a few days later to learn the fine was paid for. I
called up the IRS because I wanted to be sure, and
they confirmed that the fine had indeed been paid. I
remember distinctly hearing the voice of the IRS
agent I spoke with when I told him, "Hey, I know you
guys have a hard job and receive very little apprecia-

tion for what you do. I really appreciate you." He was shocked. The phone was silent for a moment. I felt his heart opening up, and then he said in the most genuine tone, "I really appreciate that. Thank you."

Gratitude can change your life and the lives of everyone you come in contact with. Realize that you have the power to change people's lives in a simple way. But it's a decision that takes place in your inner conversations first. You must cultivate this appreciation daily before it can make a difference in the world around you. Once you do, you will be astounded at how your world changes.

Start with simple small things. Take it slow. You don't have to come up with a million things to be grateful for. Concentrate on one thing at a time, and you will advance faster than those who try to take on too much at once. Start by taking a deep breath before you get out of bed and say thank you for your life out loud. Hold your breath for a second and say thank you to yourself in your heart. Then, as you exhale slowly, say thank you out loud a third time. This will have a residual effect. As you go about your day, notice the small things that you have and say thank you for them. As you do, imagine the people laying the pipe for your water faucet. Imagine the factory workers putting together your car as you start the engine and say thank you. If you fly, imagine designers building the airplane. If you ride the bus, imagine the bus being assembled and making its way to you. Or, as you walk to your destinations, look down at the cement and give thanks to the construction workers who laid that ground so that you don't have to walk through the dirt. Giving thanks for the small things plants a seed inside us that goes deeper than just our minds; it sends a powerful ripple effect into the lives of those around us and spreads that love. At the end of the day before you go to sleep, pick one thing to be grateful for. Feel what it was like when you drank that cup of coffee, helped that person unexpectedly, or received a gift or service. Then say to yourself in your heart the words, "I am grateful," and concentrate on that for a few minutes before you drift off to sleep. You will find that as you go on you will want to do this, and you will notice that you become even more thankful and joyful to those around you. You won't be able to wait to look for things to give thanks for, and in turn, others will experience the joy that you have and that joy will spread. There are so many things to give thanks for once we learn to shift our attention. And that joy that comes from being grateful will spread to everyone around you in a magnificent way. Master these exercises until they become habit before moving on. The next key we will look at will free up more of your attention to experience limitless joy in your life!

3. STRENGTH TO FORGIVE

*"The weak can never forgive.
Forgiveness is the attribute
of the strong."*

Mahatma Ghandi

Forgiveness is a sensitive subject with many people because it's tied to all kinds of associations. Perhaps to you, it's easier said than done. Or, because of the religious undertones some people associate with forgiveness, it might come off as something that is not agreeable to you, something that is written off as being for the weak. One of the most remarkable studies I have come across is by Psychologist Loren Toussaint. In his study he investigated 1500 adults ages 66 or older from both non-religious and religious backgrounds and measured the life-sustaining benefits of relating to an individual's view on forgiveness. The results were astounding! They measured conditional versus unconditional forgiveness, belief in God's conditional versus unconditional forgiveness, and the ability to forgive others. Then after three years, they returned to these same people and found that those who had a conditional view of forgiveness

died much sooner than those who had an unconditional view of forgiveness.

Their summary was that those who held onto demands were more likely to harbor resentment,
grudges, and emotions that can impair their heart's
health. "By continually nursing those negative feelings
it keeps your stress levels high, and it's that stress
that ultimately exacts a cost of an earlier death," says
Dr. Susan Krauss Whitbourne, Ph.D.
Why should this be so surprising? We're holding on to
that anxiety in our inner-conversations and it spreads
to every part of our system. In fact, holding on to that
wrong you feel has been done to you is actually giving
the so called wrong-doer victory because it's contami-
nating your entire system until disease sets in and
wipes you out! In his notes, Dr. Toussaint writes that
"this could reflect decades of waiting or anticipating
that the conditions might be met for them to finally get
over something." Other studies have definitively
proved that forgiveness is consistent with better heart
health, immune system and hormones. People who
forgive are much more likely to live a happy and positive life because they don't have that weight dragging
them down. What weight are you carrying around?

Not long ago I was in London for a casting meeting
with a prominent agent who represents several global
A-list movie stars. We were discussing a project we
were both very excited about that involves a character

who suffers a traumatic brain injury from a terrorist attack, and later in the story he decides to forgive his enemies. He was astounded by the reversal in the story, and then several of his junior agents began to associate it with incidents that had occurred in Paris where tragedy had just struck. They were moved by a story on the news of Antoine Leiris who lost his wife and child in this terrorist attack along with 89 other people at the Bataclan Theater; Leiris decided to forgive his enemies on worldwide television within days of the attack.

As the junior agents recounted the memory of this moving experience, I watched as this titan of show business tightened up in his chair and began to squirm with bitterness. The room fell silent. Then we exchanged a look and he said, "Not me. I would never forgive that. I prefer bitterness when it comes to things like this." He actually said those words. This is a wonderful man and an agent I highly respect and regard as a colleague. However, I was surprised at how candid he was. His perspective is understandable when you consider the atrocities that were done, and I imagine many readers will share those sentiments. Some people carry the perspective that forgiveness is for the weak or the pious, but really it is a gift for everyone.

Forgiveness is actually a gift we give ourselves. Now we're really getting into a powerful key as we honestly face our inner-conversations. We might think we've let go of animosity because we choose not to think about it, but that's not forgiveness; that's called avoidance. Facing your feelings requires courage and honesty. This is why the book began with awareness, because before you can get into some of the wonderful tools, you must be able to sit in the silence and face your thoughts and feelings. You must be willing to ask yourself, "Have I really let this go?" It's easier said than done. Once we do, there are not only extraordinary health benefits, but you will also find your relationships flourishing in a way you never thought was possible. I experienced this first hand with a traumatizing childhood event, which for years was something I was not able to let go of. It's not that I didn't want to, I just didn't know how, and it felt good sometimes to harbor bitterness for the person who I felt was responsible. Without going into too much detail, one of my close relatives was sexually assaulted in our home while I was out playing with friends after school. When our family learned of what happened, the aftershock seemed like it was largely swept under the rug. I don't remember our family ever speaking about it. It seemed like any time it was brought up, the feeling of dread swept over the room. Although, I was only in elementary school at the time, I held onto a deep seeded feeling of responsibility simply because I was not there to stop it. It seemed like a silent plague swept over our family though everyone tried to go like everything was normal. Steps were taken to pursue a legal solution for what happened, but we later learned due to the circumstances the man responsible got away. This ate away at me for years as I watched my parents' marriage dissolve slowly. I wanted to let it go more than anything in the world, but every time this man's face came to my mind I wanted to track him down and see him brought to some good old fashion vigilante justice. I couldn't bring myself to do that either.

> *"It doesn't excuse my mistakes,*
> *but I'm holding out for grace.*
> *I'm holding out that Jesus*
> *took my sins onto the cross."*

> ### *Bono, U2*

Jesus taught his followers to forgive those who have wronged you "seventy-times-seven," and to bless those who curse you. He's not the only one who taught that, but he was one to live it. Some of the greatest thinkers, artists, musicians, politicians, philosophers, and writers give credence that what Jesus's capacity to forgive is something unlike any other figure in human history. So if at this point that's all Jesus is to you, then so be it. But be careful to write him off because of any religious connotations that he represents in your mind, because that's not who he is,

that's only who he is in your mind's eye. Jesus said
He came to bring unconditional love to the world
through the forgiveness of sins. Everyone to some
extent acknowledges that the Beatles were right when
they sang the classic "All you need is love," so perhaps if the English word "Jesus" makes you uncomfortable, focus on the joy he sought to bring into the
world by forgiving even the enemies who nailed him
to the cross. That act alone is rare and miraculous!
It's interesting that leading doctors and psychologists
are catching onto the fact that forgiveness isn't just for
the spiritually pious. It's for everyone.

For over seventeen years I held onto the resentment,
hate, bitterness, and anger toward the man who
shipwrecked our family and apparently received no
justice for what he had done. During a time of meditation I remember thinking about the man who had
done this horrible act and how he may be out there
today still doing this to others and playing a part in de-
filing innocent children. Something came over me and
with sadness and anger I inquired in the silence, "Jesus, where were you when this happened?" At that
moment it was like a bolt of lightning had ran down
my spine; my eyes flooded with tears. That was a
seminal moment in my life, because I saw a vision
picture perfect clarity for the first time. I saw myself as
I walked into the bathroom where this man who had
done this horrible act was washing himself after sexually assaulting my relative. I turned around and stand-

ing behind me was the face of my Creator filled with unconditional love. Arms of bright light wrapped around me with more warmth and joy than I could ever imagine. In that moment, something changed inside me. Only weeks later, I was driving down the road and this man's face popped into my mind, but something had been forever altered in my emotion; a compassion fell over me that seemed so unthinkable before that. I actually felt compassion for this man. And there it was. I said it. No, I screamed it at the top of my lungs, "I forgive all of it!" After that moment, all hatred and bitterness was let from my veins like the tears that streamed down my cheeks. And since that moment, I've felt a freedom and a joy like never before. Not just for him, but for everyone else in my life. Holding onto that hate had been magnetizing more hate and more bitterness for others that had wronged me. Since it has had a snowball effect, it has become a natural habit to forgive those who I feel have wronged me. I no longer held onto the blame for myself, and I felt strengthened and enabled to have a meaningful conversation with my relatives for the first time in seventeen years!

"Whenever someone has offended me, I try to raise my soul so high that the offense cannot reach it."

Rene Descartes

When you hold onto a wrong that has been done, you feed it with power that can destroy you and your relationships. Not another day! Forgiveness is a key to joy given to us by our Creator and its power is limitless. Now that you're aware of what you've been giving your attention to, and you also recognize that you have many things to be grateful for, and you don't need to hold onto any more bitterness, now is the time to forgive and let go. You will not regret this. You must know when you forgive you're not endorsing the wrong that was done, but you are letting go of it for good so that joy can take its place. As the study showed, it's important not to condition forgiveness as a result of any body or anything around you changing first. That's conditional forgiveness. You must also recognize that once you do this you cannot use this wrong as leverage against anyone in the future, because that gives it power to come back and harm you as well as others you love indirectly. Once you choose to forgive, from then on you are letting it go completely. Now it's time to get down to business and use this magnificent key of forgiveness! To actually use this key, you must understand that to forgive someone you don't need to say it to their face. Most people think they must have a formal setting and a way for those words to reach their conscious mind. That is where most people get anxious because, as I did, they conjure up in their mind a scene where you say I forgive you and then you think of how they'll react or how you'd react to actually having to face them and the whole thing crumbles. Actually the opposite is true. Trying to approach someone with words face to face is looking to the external world to try and solve an internal problem.

> *"Always forgive your enemies;*
> *nothing annoys them so much."*

Oscar Wilde

First, before anything can change in a relationship, something must change through your inner-conversation. Until then, every interaction you have will still contain the thorns of bitterness and hate blocking your view. Once you've forgiven them in your heart, all things are possible in your relationships. Who is that person you're holding onto feelings about? Perhaps it's you. Have you ever thought about anything you've done that you feel the need to punish yourself for? It's not a noble thing as much as it might seem to be, and that which you're holding on to you must know could be the very thing that takes your health. But it doesn't have to. You are forgiven. It's your perspective that is cluttered, and you must know that every moment you hold onto that it clouds your ability to care for those relationships and activities in your life that you want to do right by. You will be free to bring that joy to them a hundred times as much. This is why forgiveness is not just a one-time thing. It should be a daily decision that we make as we go through our day, and certainly when those emotional alarms come up and you start feeling blame towards someone. Whether it's you or someone else, it's important to let it go before it takes root in your life and hurts someone around you unintentionally. Watchfulness is key! Now as you practice this exercise, it's important you understand this is not just a routine, it's a choice you make out of love for yourself and those around you. There are also other ways equally as effective as what I outline here, and you may develop your own method as you're inspired by this. That's great! The key is not in the conditional activity, it's what is taking place in your inner-conversation, so that joy may be come manifest in every area of your life.

> *"Forgiveness is not an occasional act, it is a constant attitude."*
>
> ### *Martin Luther King Jr.*

Find a place where you can be alone and concentrate. That might be a walk in nature, in a quiet room listening to some music, or going for a bike ride or run as I like to do. Think of one person, just one, you still have bad feelings about, and concentrate on them.

Put all of your attention on them and don't allow your attention to drift elsewhere until you have a clear picture of them in your mind. Feelings will arise. You must confront the darkness. Don't be afraid of those feelings. Face them. Perhaps you're concerned that they are still threatening you, or maybe you're tempted to think of all the ways to get back at them. Now that you have the picture of the person in your mind and the feeling associated with the wrong that has been done, ask your Creator, "Where were you when this happened?" Whether you believe in a Creator or you prefer to call it the Universe, we're talking about the same source. The Universe could not exist without the power of love. Scientists call this source energy and spiritualists submit that God is love. So if you prefer, you may inquire to the source as love. The name, which is only an identity our egos give things, is not as important as the concentration of your intention. Ask and you will receive. By asking this question, you are letting the source of all love, which formed the Universe, into this area. Ask as many times as you need to until you're satisfied. Once you have done this sufficiently, relax, and take a few deep breaths. If you need to, mentally shout their name, and then quietly to yourself in your inner dialogue, say to them in your heart, "Thank you, thank you, thank you. I forgive all and I let it go."

The reason for saying thank you in advance is it requires faith to give thanks for evidence not yet seen.

To give thanks for the forgiveness that has yet to come in your being stirs the joy inside you and prepares the soil. Next, I recommend taking some time to acknowledge all of the hurt you have felt throughout your life, so that you can make a declaration within yourself to forgive everyone who you feel has ever hurt you. You can concentrate on each individual person and say, "I forgive you," or you can simply meditate on everyone as a whole and repeat, "I forgive everyone who has ever hurt me throughout my entire life. Thank you, thank you, thank you." When you do this holding nothing back inside your entire being watch and see what happens inside your heart. It will grow in magnificent ways with joy for all people. Remember, there will naturally be times you may hit a trigger and this person or memory will creep up in your mind and tempt you to give into these destructive feelings, but the wonderful thing is the power of darkness has been eliminated, and you now have the key to banish it from your life attention forever. Rather than grabbing on to those feelings and letting them take you for a haunted house ride, realize that you can let them go! Imagine yourself crossing a peaceful stream. When you look upstream, you see a log coming toward you. The log symbolizes this unpleasant memory or person who hurt you. As that log approaches, you're tempted to grab on or let it hit you, but instead just step to the side and let it pass. It actually is that simple in practice. When you focus on that log, it will probably hit you in the eye and it will hurt! Let that log pass right on by and say, "thank you, I let it go."

This is a practice, used in post-traumatic stress therapy outlined in the PTSD Sourcebook by Dr. Glenn Shiraldi, is a wonderful technique for moving on from traumatic memories. I have studied his book and I highly recommended it for anyone who is dealing with serious trauma or is related to someone who is. When these memories do come back, do not become discouraged, remember to say, "Thank you, thank you, thank you, I forgive all, and I let it go." Watch how this key to joy fills your attention with gladness, and where there was bitterness, you'll be filled with increased vitality and strength to love even when you come up against it. You will be moved to inspire others when they are wrestling with blame or complaint when something has happened to them. You will make it a constant part of your attitude to forgive and your life will be filled with an abundance of joy that nobody can take from you. This is a precursor to one of the most amazing keys to transforming your life and your world, one that you are about to open the door to in the next chapter!

4. AWAKENED IMAGINATION

"Assume a virtue if you have it not."

William Shakespeare

It's Saturday morning 9:47 AM, and I have a 10 AM meeting a few blocks away. I'm standing in line at Staples waiting to pick up an order I needed to present at the meeting. The line is out the door, and I'm in the very back. There is only one older gentleman working the whole print area. Oftentimes, there's at least two. The way things are progressing; I probably won't be out of here until well after 10. I pride myself on being punctual. Nothing bothers me more than keeping someone waiting, because I consider my time valuable, and I feel a sense of responsibility when I make others wait even for a minute or two. I will have to send them a text to tell them I'm running late. Since it's a breakfast meeting, chances are being late means I can expect that awkward encounter where I show up and they've already ordered or worse still, completed their meal. Meetings like this seem to never get off on the right foot. I'm looking across the line at this balding man with square wire-framed glasses and few of his front teeth remaining, working the counter hunched over like life has taken it's toll on him. He's got to be in his seventies. I observe the impatient reactions from the others ahead of me giving him that look which says only one thing, "Hurry it up!" He probably would go faster if he could, but there's a sense that going any faster may very well result in a heart attack. I was filled with anxiety for fear of being late, and frustrated by these people ahead of me asking follow up questions to their follow up questions about a silly little order of newspaper clipping copies. Who needs those anyway? Buy yourself a cheap printer at home. This line is for real print orders! I don't know this clerk, although he looks vaguely familiar. Since I process almost all of my orders at Staples, chances are we've probably crossed paths. As I look up at him again something comes over me like a sixth sense, and I feel compassion for him. I imagine being in his shoes. I can actually feel what it would be like to be wearing his shoes and doing this job at his age, probably making close to minimum wage in the sage years of his life, taking demands from clients who are impatient and just want to get on their way. I realize most people probably don't care how his feet might feel or how his hands might hurt. What is it like for him to go home at the end of the day not knowing if he'll wake up again? How does he feel when he considers that he has to work this job while most people his age are out on the golf course enjoying retired life? My desire to have my order and leave on time was completely overcome by compassion for this man. I felt connected to him and it was a choice I made in that moment. I remember saying to myself something so simple, "I love you."

My imagination was suddenly flooded with sense that everything was in perfect harmony. And not a moment later this clerk looked up and past everyone in the line and made eye contact with me. He raised his voice so that I could hear it, and with at least six to eight people in front of me said, "I don't know where your ticket number is. You can just take your order and go." I couldn't believe what just happened, nor could anyone standing in the line in front of me. I looked over across the print desk and there they were. A stack of poster-sized storyboards printed and laminated. I walked over sheepishly toward them, and like a kid in a candy store, I thanked the old man with a glowing smile and I left. It was only 9:50 AM. I can still make it on time. This is remarkable. It's the simplest thing in the world, and yet in that moment it was a gigantic miracle just to pick up my order without waiting another minute and allowing me to make it to my meeting on time. Throwing out all frustration and anxiety about the whole occasion, I went to my meeting in a complete state of joy. I shared what happened with those present and they were inspired and amazed as well. This is example is a microcosm of the power that we have.

*"Don't wait for signs to live
from the state of the aim."*

Neville Goddard

When you think of the word "imagination," what thoughts come up in your mind? Perhaps you think of people who live in a dream world, not practical, responsible people. Perhaps you think of mystical hippies who live out in the Arizona desert and do drugs all day long. Maybe you think that's not something you have a lot of because you once tried to use your imagination to create something and life just didn't pan out the way you imagined. So you've done your best to accept the cards you're dealt and are moving on. You think you're too far along to use your imagination. Everyone has a certain perception about what the imagination really is. Another way to look at the imagination is to consider it from the lens of faith. What is faith? "Faith is the substance of things hoped for the evidence of things unseen," as the writer of Hebrews put it. It seems on the one hand, you have loads of people who know they need faith, and on the other hand, multitudes who love what can come from the human imagination, say from Walt Disney or Steve Jobs. And in between, very few people who actually understand that the same imagination or faith that Walt Disney and Billy Graham exercised is the ability that you have access to!

What is the imagination and how do you use it? The reality is that everyone uses their imagination throughout their life and many do it unknowingly. Imagination is the ability to envision something that is unseen to your eye and believe that it is already accomplished in reality. It's the ability to actually feel the joy for something that you don't have yet. When you substitute this for the word faith you can see how really it's the same activity used for different purposes. Someone can use this for good or evil purposes. That is the power that we have been given. Imagination is like a muscle and it strengthens with exercise. Someone who uses it constantly may have the capability of an Olympic athlete, where someone who lets it atrophy may have trouble just getting out of bed to eat breakfast. Whether you use it well or use it foolishly, we all have access to it. God has given it to us. When you really consider what prayer is and what is actually happening, you see that it is expressing a desire to an infinite Creator. To use this great key of imagination, the real secret is believing in the unseen, that the desire you have has already been fulfilled before any signs are reflected in your outer world. This is not a matter of wishful thinking, neither is it a matter of just saying, "I'd like to have my legs working, and I've been saying it for a long time and nothing is happening, so all this faith and imagination stuff is hogwash!" That's not using your imagination, that's expressing doubt, and confirming it over and over again. Your life is the way it is because that's what you've expected to see. Those are preconceptions you've set up in your mind, and of course you look for everything in your outer world to verify that's true. You say, "I'm this way because I was born into this environment, and these are the limited opportunities handed to me, and I'm doing the best I can." This goes back to your inner conversations. What are you telling yourself? When you are really using your imagination, you are actually transcending your circumstances, including the messages you've been feeding to yourself. You are putting your faith in the unseen.

You certainly can use your imagination to create wonderful things in your environment. Many criticize this as being of the nature of prosperity theology. That's just limited thinking. If that's the case, you'd have to put Jesus and almost every other revered spiritual figure in that category as well, because he conducted miracles, such as multiplying bread and wine. We all have access to that same gift today. The key is Jesus exercised that power out of love, not for selfish or greedy purposes! When you use the power of imagination for greedy, hurtful or selfish purposes, it comes back to hit you like a boomerang. That should not discourage you from using your imagination, it should encourage you! When your imagination develops, and it will, watch how you are motivated to be more generous and compassionate then you've ever been before. Once you have exercised your imagination, have faith and experience the joy as if you've already realized your desire. But, it must be said, you should be careful to not boast about it. Once the reality of what you have imagined has made its way into the world and the proof is there, allow others to celebrate what has happened. They will see with their own eyes. Until then, in your inner-conversations, give thanks that the seed has been planted. God's ways are mystifying, so it is not up to you to try and use your willpower to bring about what only your Creator knows. You don't need to know how it will happen, only that it has happened. As for how long it takes, that is really a matter of how much faith you have that it is already done. It could happen immediately or it could take time, but one thing is for sure, you must feel and know that it is already done. If you hope to travel to Africa with a charitable organization to build wells, or make a certain amount of money so that you can give more to a cause you believe in, you must fully believe that it is already an accomplished fact, and you are not looking for validation without for it to come about. I often hear people say, "Well my goal is to do such and such if things fall into place." You must watch out for the word "if," for it is a subtle way of expressing doubt that it will come about. You must remove the word "if" from your vocabulary. This re-quires watchfulness. Many people will sit alone in a room and imagine themselves doing what they love, having the car, the house, or even changing the world, but once they go back to daily life, they allow the expectations of the world to sweep away their faith. They allow the environment they now inhabit to dictate what they believe. Remember your current circumstances are a result of an accumulation of past beliefs. You don't believe that? Consider the high school student who is expected to go to college. They put their attention on earning the grades. They are expected to secure a reasonable job. They take out the necessary loans or use family resources to get through college to secure a degree that will allow them to practice whatever they set out to do and eventually retire. They might say they never set out to be a desk clerk or lawyer, but what was the existing belief or expectation that they had? Perhaps it was a desire to have security or to be respected or to be loved. That controlling desire has shaped the circumstances you now inhabit. This is an accumulation of beliefs and thinking which begins as a seed inside each person from a very young age. Now you find yourself with a desire to imagine a life that you want to live, be it noble or selfish, that desire is there. What is the key to actually manifesting that desire in your world? The secret is living from the state of the aim at all times. Have the faith. Feel the joy of doing that regardless of what your outer circumstances currently dictate. Remember, it is best to not talk about the desire or to try to prove to others around you that you're doing this, or that you're going to do this. This will not help you. In fact, by trying to prove it, others are likely to confront you, saying that your desire is not going to happen. They will try to convince you that it's not reasonable and that you might as well put your attention on something that is practical. It is most important to give thanks for it and believe morning, noon, and night, both in your feelings and your thoughts that it is already done. Do not worry about how it will come about, simply give thanks that it has been done. You can certainly use this ability to manifest things in your world as a testament of faith. There's nothing wrong with having a wonderful life that allows you to do charitable things for others. It has been said by Jesus to forget not the poor. How can you help the poor if you have nothing to give them? That being said, the highest way to use this power is for others. When you do this, you will watch your imagination grow and strengthen, because it will give you joy to see others benefit. That joy will return to you multiplied in ways you cannot even begin to imagine. Let's say your goal is to imagine a certain amount of money, but you maintain a belief that money is bad and only for the greedy. When that money comes, is it going to make you happy?

"There is nothing either good or bad, but thinking makes it so."

William Shakespeare

There is nothing wrong with having money, but it should never become the focus, because money is a means to an end. Money is an assignment of value. What do you value? The highest way to use your imagination is for the love of others, and that in return gives you unending joy. If money and possession are what you value, and you consist of infinite energy, how will your soul feel when it's ready to leave this body? Probably empty. It's wonderful to create miracles and opportunities so long as they are driven by an intention which transcends what we can see, feel and touch. Why? That's the key to joy, because joy enables you to transcend your circumstances.

Think about how you will feel once you manifest that car of your dreams. You will likely want something else and that cycle is endless. However, when you use your imagination for the benefit of others, watch out, everything inside of you will be empowered like never before, and you will be supercharged with faith to live with that joy. The key to your imagination that I present to you is rooted in compassion, and I guarantee it works! You might ask what if I sit down in that chair and imagine myself fully doing this wonderful thing, having everything I need to do it. I can see the faces of those around me celebrating that this has come about, and yet nothing has happened. What do I do? I would answer you that something has happened, and it happened inside you. If it you really believe something is growing then it's already bearing fruit, because that joy is going to influence you and every relationship you have. As for when it will be fully realized in your environment, it's enough to know that it will.

"Without a vision, people perish."

Proverbs 29:18

Have you looked at your skin, your age, your circumstances, and thought I'm past having a vision, I'm just going to live with what I got? Do you know that complacency or laziness is not something to be proud of? Some people are proud of how they put their stock in what they can see. You're not too old or too poor to dream! You don't need anything outside yourself to have a dream and to watch your Creator bring it about. You were made in the image and likeness of God. You're not just a meat suit. Those hands and legs are instruments. What you really are is an infinite soul capable of doing the most magnificent things the world has ever seen. Yes! Not some other reader - I'm talking about you! There's something you dreamed of being or doing when you were young, and it got stepped on by the world because somebody or something confronted that dream, and it was put away for a time. It's time to live your dream! That doesn't mean you have to quit your job and move somewhere. You've got what it takes to use your imagination right where you are. You might say I don't have time with all the responsibilities I have to dream, that's for those ungrounded foolish kids out West. You are actually not too different. You just haven't awakened your imagination, so you're stuck to your circumstances. Whether you have a dependable blue-collar job or a respectable portfolio of investments, if you're still unhappy it's likely that you haven't experienced the joy of awakening your imagination! "Dreams are the seedlings of reality," pens James Allen in his marvelous book, As A Man Thinketh. So what are you dreaming about? Are you living your life like a zombie based on an uncontrolled imagination? Have you ever felt that you were capable of doing something, but it was out of harmony with your circumstances, so you dismissed it? I am proof you can achieve your dreams.

Eight years ago, I was living month to month in a house I had rented from my sister, and we were really struggling just to cover the bare minimum. I had written a script for a film I really wanted to make which I felt could touch the whole world, but I had no resources to make it or the studio leverage to green light this film. I understood the power of the imagination had driven me to write this screenplay, but the vast majority of screenplays written by aspiring young filmmakers are never made. Everything in my world shouted you are not going to make this movie! I recall a time when my agent sent the script to an executive at Sony Pictures only to have him come back saying, "This isn't for us. Thanks and best of luck." I was crushed! I felt there was no hope for me to ever get this film made. One night I was imagining premiering this film in the prestigious Academy Theater in New York City, and I went online to find a picture of this empty theater with all the Oscar statues around. I knew that some of the greatest filmmakers like Martin Scorsese screened his movies there, and I wanted more than anything just to play my film there when it was complete. I felt deeply this film was one that could inspire those suffering from persecution to per- severe against all odds. I put this picture of the Acad- emy Theater on my desktop, and every time I looked at it I imagined myself introducing my film at the re- lease. A few years later, a financier came to me from out of the blue and funded the entire film and the prints and advertising costs to release the film theatri- cally in over 736 theaters. One of his requirements for underwriting the film was that we hold a premiere in New York City. As we approached the release date for the film, I received an email from the publicists. They said we had a couple recommendations as for where we should hold the premiere, and one of these three was the Academy Theater in New York City! I leaped with joy and confirmed that is where I'd like to hold it. On July 18, 2014 the film was received at a red carpet premiere in New York City, and I introduced the film to the world with tremendous joy and satisfac- tion. That's not all, within a few months of the release, I received an offer from Sony Pictures to carry the release of the film internationally to over 30 countries around the world. This was the same studio who has said they were not interested before. I had no influence on how the Academy Theater came into the conversation or how Sony Pictures entered my environment, I only imagined that these things would take place.

Our Creator's ways are unfathomable to us. You have this power within you no matter what background you come from or what circumstance you find yourself in. Take some time alone either in a quiet room or take a walk in nature and ask yourself these questions. Before you consider these questions, I would remind you for this to be fruitful, they ought to be in line with the Golden Rule, "Doing unto others as you would have them do unto you." Now fully imagine what you would feel like if your heart's desire were to have been accomplished now. Ask yourself how would you feel? Who would you tell with joy that it has happened? What would be the reactions on their faces? What would you do as a result? How would you feel spreading that joy to others? Now imagine yourself going through your daily routine with this joy of having already accomplished your desire. As you bump into people or circumstances that would ordinarily make you uncomfortable, feel the joy that you have inside you. Let it permeate your entire being. Anytime the feeling rises inside, you say "thank you" for that desire being accomplished. When doubt tries to creep in and tell you that you're lying to yourself and this will never happen, cast it out with light by giving thanks for what you already have! Do this morning, noon, and night. As it has been said by Jesus, "Pray without ceasing." When you pray or meditate believing you have received your desire by faith, you are mediating with your Creator. Before we move onto that, remember as you're exercising your imagination in your infancy stages, don't try to lift a fifty-pound kettle bell. You've got what it takes, and you have the key to gratitude. Anytime you begin to doubt because you see something in your external world that challenges this dream, pull out the key of gratitude and find something to give thanks for. This could be the smallest thing in the world like the breath in your lungs, or the shoes on your feet. This key will be instrumental to you as you begin to exercise your imagination because it will cast out doubt. You will start to recognize the joy you're already grateful for. One of the most powerful and miraculous ways to use this gift is for the good of others, and this will multiply your joy and your ability to use your imagination like an Olympian, which is where we're headed in the next chapter... so take this step today and never give up!

5. SHARE THE WEALTH

*"We make a living by what we get,
but we make a life by what we give."*

Winston Churchill

Have you ever met an unhappy generous person? I haven't. This is not a lesson about the guilt of giving intended to make you feel bad about what you're making and using for your needs. The opposite is true! In fact, the more you give the more that comes back to you. This is about the joy of giving. Many miss out on this wonderful joy and they think they would rather have that money than this joy. Statistically, 33% of Americans give nothing away, and yet America remains the most generous country in the world giving away 300 billion annually to foreign aid. A majority of that aid comes through private individuals, superseding government aid. Still, 63% of American individuals earning under $25,000 a year do not give away money at all. America's giving is only 2% of the GDP, which is still twice as high as the Canadians and 20 times as high as developing countries. Why give when you can keep all those bills to yourself? John D. Rockefeller put it this way, "I have made many millions, and they have brought me no happiness." How could that be? Generosity is a key. I'm so excited to share, because it has brought my wife and I more joy than I ever expected. It's the key to joy, which frees you from your circumstances!

We think we want money, but what we really want is happiness. We think money will bring us happiness, but the irony is that giving it away is what actually brings us the most joy. The act of generosity, giving and expecting nothing in return, actually multiplies those resources and through unexpected means brings you more joy and more resources than you imagined. Lots of people say, "I would give, but I barely have enough money right now to make ends meet. Once I make my millions, then I'll start giving." Let me tell you right now, you wont. Giving is not about the amount of money at all. You might have ten dollars to your name and you see someone on the street who needs it. You give them five dollars knowing that the other five you will give to your child so that they can eat. This might mean that you will go hungry. That act of generosity could be worth more than Rockefeller giving away a million dollars. Do you see why? Money is only a means. It's an assignment of value. It's a concentration of energy and power to do something, not the end itself.

"You couldn't pay me enough not to give."

Randy Alcorn

Having great wealth is not a bad thing. It is your birthright. I am one who believes there's a great joy in being productive, taking care of your loved ones, and using those resources to bring joy to others. Money is a tool, and it must have a purpose. When you become wealthy and prosperous, those resources were entrusted to you. You might have built up in your mind that having a big boat and five cars inside your palatial mansion is what would bring you joy. In reality, having those resources and using them to help others along the way will actually bring you more joy than all the material possessions in the world. There's nothing wrong with having the things you need at all! I love cars, and I marvel at the engineering and the love put into them. I enjoy what they do for people. I love to run, so I like to have good shoes to run in. Why would our Creator give us feet if he didn't' want us to walk or run? Naturally, it's great to enjoy the things we have, but there's a secret within that understanding: we have to enjoy it with an open hand! When you become fixated on the stuff to bring you joy, it will disappoint because that stuff wears out and you need new stuff to make you happy. When you make bringing joy to others a goal through generosity, you can enjoy the stuff without it owning you. That's the trick. When someone needs a new pair of shoes or you notice you have an extra pair, you're thrilled to give them away, knowing they will make someone else happy. Joy multiplies because the people you help are inspired to do that for someone else. The same is true with our time and financial resources. When we give, it's not a loss, it's an investment, and in fact, it's the smartest investment on the planet. Some people think they cannot afford to give, because they are not giving. If you can come up with excuses as to why you're not giving now, those excuses will only be compounded when you have more. As long as you come from a place of lack, you'll always live in that state. It's those who are faithful in the small things that are made rulers over many things. Every time you give generously, you move a fulcrum in the unseen world, which moves mountains both in your faith and in the world around you. It's a joy to give, and it's not about the amount of money. It's the motive behind it. That doesn't mean you should give less, because it's not about the amount. It means we should give more even above our comfort zone. You will receive in measure with what you give. Giving has a way of breaking our orbit around our possessions to see the joy in life. It connects us with those people and causes that we love. It brings us into a place of joy, because now we've become a giver and not a taker. When you put yourself into harmony as a giver, you raise your frequency to place of love for others, and the joy that forms inside you is imperishable. It transcends circumstances and possessions. Show me your bank statements, and I'll show you your heart. Now that you've felt the joy of gratitude as part of your life, you're ready to use your key of imagination to experience the joy of giving generously. This must start from within, not without. We ought to never give out of guilt or pressure from others. It must be done out of love from within. I believe in both giving regularly and spontaneously. I started my journey of charity with giving away 10% of everything I made even when I was stretched financially, and I didn't know where our groceries were coming from. Every time without fail, the resources came in, year after year. I never missed a payment, and we have excellent credit. I've made it a goal to give away 50% of everything I make and to give spontaneously when I am able to. I am driven to do this not out of guilt but a growing desire to transform the world with joy. You can too! I was in the same position as many of you, struggling to make ends meet month to month. Out of my desire to bring joy to others, I've been entrusted with more resources to take care of our needs and the needs of others. We are filled with unending joy when we see lives and pictures of the children impacted that we are helping in underprivileged neighborhoods around the world. It has opened doors for us to serve food and supplies to the homeless and to teach our young children about the joy of generosity with first hand experience. I'll never forget the look on my three year old boy when he got to click the mouse and send money to our sponsor child in Africa. We've made it a tradition to serve as many others at the homeless shelter on Thanksgiving. Our boys do get a little hungry, but it is well worth the joy of seeing them hand a meal to homeless child with nothing. It changes you. It's been said when you serve the homeless, you are literally giving directly to the face of God. I can tell you from experience that's exactly how it feels. How could it be there are so many people missing out on this joy? Maybe they are afraid they will get hurt or become like them. The truth is we are all like them, and they like us. We are all children. Every single peddler we ever judged was once a child with hopes and dreams. Surely if you could rewind the clock and see that boy or girl for the child they are, you would not judge them so harshly. Next time you see a homeless person on the street, instead of judging them, imagine them as they might have looked as a child. Look at them and see them that way and your heart will be moved with compassion to pray for them. Whether you have money to give or not you can send them your joy with a kind look. That's not just a look. Your heart emits powerful vibrations, and it's a fact that when you send bitter or loving thoughts, they make a difference. Try this simple technique, and you will be moved with joy the next time you see that child holding out a cardboard sign begging for food!

"Joy is a sign of generosity. When you are full of joy, you move faster and you want to go about doing good to everyone."

Mother Teresa

Why is America's giving only at 2%, which is twice as high as any other nation? When you have money and you hold onto it, whether it's a vast sum or a few hundred dollars, there's a tendency to clench up with fear someone is going to take it. Whether you're on the high or low spectrum of the income chart, take some time alone in a quiet room or in nature and imagine one person or organization that you would love to help. Don't concern yourself with how much or how it might result in you lacking in resources. Simply concentrate on the feeling and thought of helping them. When you really do this, a feeling of joy will come. Hunches will come on what to do and who to give to and the amount will not concern you. Usually, you will have faith to give more than you did when you were stuck in your own ego trying to sort everything out intellectually. You might ask if it is a requirement to give regularly or spontaneously. There's wisdom to giving first on every cent of income before you spend on yourself, because it sets a tone of putting others first. Then when you feel compelled to give spontaneously, don't question it. Experience the joy of giving and watch how it brings you more joy in your life and relationships than you ever had in the bank. When you give generously, it brings about a change in consciousness. It brings you into a place of joy. Suddenly you look at what you have, and you feel grateful. We're all connected by an infinite Creator, and when we give, we're actually experiencing a connection and joy with the party we gave to, so we're not losing at all. Every time I have given with a joyful heart, sooner or later I look back and everything I gave has come back, "pressed down and shaken together with good measure," as scripture says. That means I received back more than I gave. The intent is not to get something back, but you cannot out give our Creator. I love to keep each of the organizations and individuals I've given to in my thoughts throughout the day, and each time I think of them, I give thanks for the tremendous joy it brings. Sometimes it's just the fuel you need to persevere through a challenging time. When you're nearing the end of your life, and you're thinking about how are you going to feel about what you did with it? When you give generously that energy multiplies, and it has no end. The joy of giving never runs dry, and it is the only investment to never perish. So as you go back to your life, whether you have a massive bank balance or not enough to pay your bills, consider this, and imagine yourself giving generously with your thoughts. Out of joy, determine what you'd like to give and say in your inner-conversation in silence, "Thy will be done." Your intention will be heard and with the key of generosity watch how your joy grows. Concentrate on helping others, one person at a time. Your joy will grow and multiply. You will be astounded like the boy who was willing to give his few loaves of bread and fishes, which were multiplied to feed the multitudes. Your joy will be so full and overwhelming, you won't even recognize yourself. How silly mere money seeking appears in the presence of a generous heart, serene and beautiful. Your Creator loves a cheerful giver! If as you pursue the joy of generosity in your heart, thorns of anxiety stand in your way, say unto your heart, 'Peace, be still!" Once you have taken the first step on your own journey of generosity, you're ready to receive the master key!

6. YOUR IMAGINARY WORLD

"As a man thinketh in his heart so he is."

Proverbs 23:7

For a moment, imagine you're an Olympic athlete competing in the open 400 meter dash in a few weeks. You will be representing your country, going up against the fastest, most well-trained runners in the entire world. You have been training for this moment your entire life. You cut everything out of your diet and lifestyle that could impede your performance in any way. Coaches and trainers watch you around the clock. Doctors sit you down and wire you up to monitors in a dark room to measure every inch of your body and mind. They tell you to close your eyes and imagine yourself running the race now. They tell you to get in the starting blocks, feel the gun go off, thrust yourself into gear, envision yourself charging toward the finish line, and feel it all like it's happening at this very moment. You do. You feel and see every single aspect so clearly sweat begins to drip from your temples. It takes on all the tones of reality. As you give every last ounce of strength on the final hundred yard stretch, you don't let up, instead you kick it into high gear, absorbing near supernatural strength, and you overtake the lead, winning the race. The crowd goes wild. You have won the Olympics! You're a world champion runner. The doctors tell you it's alright to open your eyes. The feeling was so real you have difficulty believing your senses. You're sitting in a clinical testing room. This can't be reality. I know I'm standing at the finish line of the Olympics. That feels more real than this does. You look down and behold the wires attached to your body, which trail up to computer monitors. The doctor reads the feedback and looks ecstatic. He simply turns his head to you and smiles, "You did it!" The feedback confirms that your brain fired off exactly the same responses that you would if you actually ran the race.

"I sat for hours and imagined what my reason denied until those around me became players in my imaginary world."

Neville Goddard

In this life you will face trials and hardships. It's inevitable. Things and forces will confront you from the outside world, which will tempt you to return to former ways. They will lure you to give into hate and return evil with evil. Man has distorted and used this wonderful gift to imagine all kinds of evils, too. These are things we see in the news and in our daily lives. The secret key to trials is not to live in a state of protest or reaction to them. Most people live their lives reactively. They see something or hear something or run into a conflict and they turn into a pinball bouncing from one thing to the next until they pass on from this life. You have the secret. However, knowing what to do and actually doing it is a whole different matter. People know that prayer and meditation is a higher way than to use force, but few have the courage to do it. When a man or woman tries to change the world around them without first changing their own self within, it is a futile readjustment of surfaces. It will not last. There are practical and applicable methods for making it a habit to focus within regardless of what difficulties may confront you. First, it's essential to understand that you must never under any circumstance use this great gift to imagine evil against someone. When you do this evil will come back on you multiplied. We have a responsibility to imagine what is pure, lovely, and of good report. We must never entertain an unlovely thought. We must never entertain lust or greed, because even though those pleasures might seem lovely on the surface, we know that the results of those pleasures reap only the whirlwind of harm to ourselves, and others around us. You will confront these temptations, because we are all tempted. Do not criticize or come down on yourself for being tempted, for even the greatest men and women of virtue who have ever lived have endured temptation to imagine evil. Cast it aside and look forward to the prize. Remember what you focus on grows. Do not allow hate to consume your thoughts, because it will bring you down. If you allow yourself to be against something in protest, your attention falls with that very thing you protest. Live in an atmosphere of meditation instead of a state of force or protest. When you come up against troublesome circumstances that seem so real and insurmountable to you, you may want to resort to using force. Do not give into this. If there's an outer threat, we must look within. These threats are the appearance of reality, but these things are in reality a shadow of the past. It is the soul inside you, which is more real than anything around you. All the statues and monuments in the museums in the world combined have less power than the soul inside your being.

"Our deepest fear is not that we are inadequate. Our deepest fear is that we are powerful beyond measure."

Marianna Williamson

You have the power of love in your heart, which is the greatest power in the Universe. You must only learn to use it. When these so-called enemies and obstacles confront your awareness, stop and turn within. This is where unlimited power is found to transcend any circumstance that you will encounter. What are you encountering right now that seems insurmountable? It is only a transformation in consciousness that will result in a change or environment and behavior. Are you relying on an outside force to come to you magically to present the solution to your problems? That will never come! There is no force on its way. This book can only open your eyes to it, but unless you make a decision to the reality of the power you have and practice it every moment of every waking day, no lasting change will occur. Do you look to the lottery to solve your financial problems? Most people who win end up broke, because they still have a poverty mentality within their own being. No change will last unless it's a change originating from within. This is why it is essential to never judge anyone else based upon appearances. God is no respecter of persons. It's foolishness. Imagine you had a meeting with the leader of Enron the day before the corporate scandal broke into public awareness. You would have likely been amazed had you been aware of this man's net worth. If you judged based on appearances, you might have treated him like a king. Let's say you walk out of that skyscraper and you pass a homeless person on the streets. Who are you more likely to pay more respect to, the bum on the streets or the CEO of a multi-million dollar corporation? It's likely that most people would treat the CEO with more respect, because of how much wealth and power he appears to have. However, at that moment only few may have known this CEO had used his imagination to do evil and would soon be taken into handcuffs and put in prison with less power and wealth than the bum on the streets. You see things can appear one way, and in reality, be something else entirely. You now have the secret key to never judge on appearances. All throughout history people have risen and fallen with the tides of consciousness. Always look within. As you begin to use these keys outlined within this book, you will surely gain the power and ability to achieve great wonders, and the world will marvel at your ability to manifest harmonious relationships and marvelous circumstances. It's pivotal to understand, as riches and pleasures increase, do not ever set your heart on them. Do not ever place your stock in your circumstances. Why? Circumstances are bound to change. You may cherish the wonderful things in life along with the hardships as long as your constant joy is sourced from within you. You must constantly have at your disposal all of the keys leading up to trials, because when you face trials, as you surely will, it may be expedient to draw upon each one of these keys and press forward to the prize. Before you do anything, you must stop to imagine the outcome. Like the Olympic runner before the world championships, feel every aspect of the race you're about to run like it's happening now and go all the way to the end. Experience the joy of the fulfillment of the goal. Concentrate on it. Go over it as many times as is needed, and it will become a reality. Do you think your Creator gave you the ability to do this, so you could use it every now and again in between intervals of bouncing around not knowing which direction you're headed? So many people acknowledge there's a creator, but they are waiting for God to tell them what to do. You have been given a mind to think and an awareness to utilize it. Do you not know we are children of the living God? If that's true, it's impossible to back track into sheepish perspective. The key is to seek validation internally and ensure everything you'd imagine to be done follows the golden rule. Is there someone or something that is aggravating you right now? In using this key of transcendence, I'd like you to pick just one situation that is problematic in your life presently. Perhaps this is one you know you can't handle by force. Maybe it's something you blame on the other party, so it's out of your hands, and it can't be resolved short of a miracle. You have thought it over and festered on it. You have done what you can, but it's not going anywhere. Or maybe it's something looming on the horizon that you feel is going to confront you. Focus on that one problem. Now I'd like you to get out a piece paper and pen and write down three things that would have to occur to reach your miraculous outcome. These three things occurring should bring you joy. Go to the end of the situation like it's happening right now in your imagination. Imagine telling a friend the news that this situation has been resolved and these three wonderful things that came from it. Now write down these three things like they've already occurred, and after you write these three things down read over them carefully. Don't rush from one to the next. Read them slowly like they have occurred and say "thank you," from within, feeling the joy of these things having happened as you go through each one. Close your eyes and see these things happening now and allow yourself to experience the joy of the miraculous outcome with this situation. Now keep this paper in a place where you'll see it throughout the day. Anytime you come across it, read each one and give thanks for the outcome with this situation or person. It's important to keep this confidential, because even with the best intentions, others may try to analyze the situation from the outside and plant seeds of doubt. As you think about it throughout the day, your mind may try to figure out how this could come about. It's not for you to know how it will come about, it's only important that you know it will. Your reasoning mind may try to say, "well, if this and this come about, maybe this will work out." At those moments, just move your attention from there and give thanks for the outcome. "If" is a very subtle way of doubt creeping in. The word "if" should be completely removed from your vocabulary in order to allow words that conform to your aim. If it's a fact in your consciousness that it has been accomplished, it will externalize. Just be sure you don't uproot the seed you've planted. When this situation is resolved, people around you will use analysis and explanations to say, "well of course this happened, because you did this and this over a period of time." They will try to make sense of it by outside explanations. You will know why it happened, but don't brag about it. Do not put them down, because they don't understand. In success, it is crucial to remain humble in all matters. You may repeat this exercise once you watch what this powerful key can do, but I would urge you to concentrate on just one situation or person to start. Once you have made a habit of doing this, you will do it automatically. You may not always write them down, but it is a great way to keep a record in a journal, as I love to do, so that when it is complete, you can write down, "Thank you!" Use this key often, and you will have the power to do so without ceasing!

7. FEELING IS THE SECRET

"The only reason for time is so that everything doesn't happen all at once."
Albert Einstein

Have you met that person who always seems to have a new great idea, but never seems to follow through in completing anything? Maybe that's you, and that's about to change. You may have been committed to a few goals, but when nothing seems to come together the way you hoped, you get discouraged and give up. That is about to change! Open your eyes as you read these pages and you will see why that is. You don't need to get any of your validation from the external world, because that is only a reflection of past thinking. If you wait for validation from the outside world, you will repeat a viscous cycle and never progress. This is wonderful news for those who are open to taking upon themselves the responsibility to commit to one goal, whatever it maybe, and remain with it, whatever may come from the world around you. The key to commitment is living the state of the aim at all times. Don't concern yourself with how it will externalize yourself. What you must concern yourself with is your internal commitment to the goal and believing that it is already a reality within you. Once that is certain, you will not be concerned about those validations, because you will now trust that it will come to pass. It always does. Let's say my desire is to bring joy to others all over the world everywhere I go all of the time. How would it work if I waited until others told me that I have brought them joy to commit to that within myself. That's insanity! And yet that is how much of the world operates. People want to bring something valuable into the world, and they are working a job they hate or living a lifestyle they detest, giving into choices they resent, while they wait for someone to hand them a lottery ticket or a contest that says, "Congratulations! Here's your ticket to the life of your dreams." People have the idea of doing some great thing, while they have not commitment or staying power to walk by faith in that state before any validation materializes. You know better now! You are being given a key to the unseen world. When you have the faith to believe in a desire of your heart, while it is still invisible to the world around you, you will be able to move mountains for it to come to pass. I could tell you countless stories, and I've shared a few throughout this book that would verify this, but that's not going to change your mind unless you make that move within yourself! Why is that? It's because every one of us has a reasoning mind which is designed to deal with the outside world. This is not a bad thing, once we understand it's purpose. Your reasoning mind makes sense of what it observes. It is limited though by what it can see and assimilate through sensory perceptions. Your heart or subconscious is the gateway to the infinite Creator, which gave us life. The key here is to not just to exercise imagination when we are in the quiet place of our mediations. Our heart and conscious mind must be in harmony. This is where most people will say, "I don't know if I can do that." It's not so complicated when you think about it in small matters. Let's say you're planning a vacation to the Bahamas. Before you go to sleep, your mind naturally conjures up images of what it will feel like when you get there. What are you going to do once you get to the hotel? How long will the flight take? You'll naturally go through those areas in your imagination. The next day, when you pack for your trip, the external world will be in harmony with your vision. It is no different when it comes to your goal! Whether it happens quickly or it takes time isn't really as important as whether you've fully committed yourself internally every moment throughout your day to live the state of the aim. This doesn't mean you have to quit your job or school to achieve this. You may be working in circumstances that are uncongenial at the moment, and you can still live the state of the aim in your awareness throughout the day. This will in fact bring joy to what were previously menial activities, and in all likelihood, raise your game. Let's say that your dream is to run in the Olympics, and right now you're only in high school on the junior varsity team. I guarantee that if you imagine yourself running in the Olympics now every single day, you would work harder, treat others better, push further, eat better, and give more in your daily life than ever before. Starting to get the picture? You have got what it takes. You've got to have both a wish-bone and a back bone. Not only that, but they must be coordinated. What happens when you try to push yourself too hard physically and your muscles haven't been properly stretched and conditioned? You're likely to injure yourself, and if you keep doing it your ability to try will decline. Let's say that your dream is to speak in front of millions of people and become president of the United States so that you can bring peace to the world. That's a wonderful dream to have. Using the analogy of the runner, should you step into the ring on a debating platform before you're prepared with one of the most experienced politicians? It's going to get ugly, and you're likely to get discouraged about trying again. That's why it's so important not to try and use force to rush things into happening too soon or to worry about how it is going to happen. You may do this and do it again and still see no difference happening in the world around you. You may fail as even the most talented do on occasions. What is the key? Always get back up and try again. Throw yourself fully into the task at hand like there is nothing else in the world of any importance. Too many people ruin their lives with distractions and scattered energies. They cannot make up their minds. If that has been you, it's time to make a decision and don't wait for your friend or spouse or colleagues to confirm you're good at it or it's your destiny to make that decision. That is the way of fools.

You have to make a choice within you about what singular goal that is so clear and so definitive that no matter what obstacle, the feeling of having achieved it will overcome any discouragement that comes your way. This is your choice. I recommend this goal is not contingent upon things or people, because people have their own will and things lose their value. This goal should be of good report and in line with the golden rule. Once you have made up your mind, go to the end and imagine an event that would take place after the fulfillment of this goal. It could be a celebration of your achievement. Imagine every detail of it. You may wish to imagine this over and over again until it becomes real. As you go about your day, give thanks to your Creator for bringing it about. You may want to do something to force it into action as you see reminders of it in the outside world. In reality, you can do nothing to force it into happening. When it does come, it will be effortless, because it wasn't your conscious mind that forced it into happening. Throw your full self into the joy of it already being fulfilled, but as you go about your day, you don't talk about it or gloat or boast about anything. You simply give thanks for the desire and live in that joyful state doing unto others as you would have them do unto you. One day you will find that your circumstances that have for so long held you back have naturally changed and come into harmony with your desire. You will likely be so humbled when this happens, you will fall on your knees and give thanks to God. Consider the time leading up to the birth of Jesus when there was talk of a coming Messiah in the land of Israel. There were people who were looked upon as highly devout and religious, esteemed in the eyes of men. The Roman Empire ruled the land. The Pharisees and the Romans alike were concerned this might disrupt the political and religious structure. Nevertheless, living hundreds of miles away in a foreign land, the Zoroastrians were convinced by faith there was a coming Messiah that would free people. They followed a star all the way across the desert to find this baby in the city of Bethlehem. What is remarkable is that there was no room for this baby in the city of Bethlehem, so Joseph and Mary had no choice but to have their child in a barn. Whether you agree or disagree with who Jesus is, it's undeniable that his life has certainly changed history thousands of years after he died a thankless death between a thief and a murderer. The people of the day seemed to be so wrapped up in their circumstances and customs that they overlooked something that a couple of Zoroastrians, who today would be perceived as new age mystics, had the faith and wisdom to recognize. Some of the thoughts and ideas presented in this book may challenge your way of looking at things. That is not reason to dismiss what you learn. In fact, what is being presented is a complete paradigm shift from the ways of the world, which operate on a materialistic way of viewing things from the outside in. At first blush, one may label something as being mystical, religious, self-help, or what have you, but the truth is not in the labels. Those are conventions that will only satisfy your ego. The truth is found only in the doing. When you encounter obstacles and adversity, you will be faced with a choice. Will I cling to my former ways, or seek the seed of joy by triumphing over adversity in this moment? I urge you to seek the seed of joy within, because any adversity can be transformed into an imperishable treasure by searching within... "Greater is He who is within you than He who is in the world." When you come up against inevitable trials in life, look for things to love in the small things. Remember what you focus on grows. The more you give attention to your problems, the more they are bound to expand. This is a matter of perception. When you are tempted to criticize, bite on your tongue, take a breath, and search for anything to give thanks for. The more you concentrate on the joy in you and all around you, the more the joy will flood into your problems and wash them away. You are the person you desire to be at this moment. You were drawn to this book because something inside you told you that you were worth more. Something spoke to you in that still small voice, telling you that you were called to more. You were! You're more extraordinary than you know, and you have within you the ability to transform the world with joy. Anyone who says you're dreaming and you've got to come back down to earth is only echoing their own insecurity. Don't accept it. Don't let that doubt in. Not ever. You have something inside you and it's imperishable.

> *"Genius is 1% inspiration*
> *and 99% perspiration."*

Thomas Edison

You could be the next President of the United States, the next founder of Apple Computers, the next Billy Graham, the next Mother Teresa, the next Martin Luther King Jr., the next Albert Einstein, the next Thomas Edison. You could be the next one of any of these. Where would our world be if they had given up on their dreams? All the cynics and skeptics in your life today who benefit from the light Thomas Edison brought would remain in darkness. You've got to keep going no matter what they say and never, ever, ever give up. You have got to keep going because there's not somebody else out there to do the work that you've got to do. Nobody else was made with your brushstrokes. Nobody else can do the work that you were made to do. Nobody else is like you at all. You feel like you're made to run? You better run with all your heart. You feel you were made to invent? You better not half-ass it. You feel you were made to act on camera? You had better wake up every single morning whether you have an audition or not and give it your best, because there's nobody else who can give the performance that you can. So there's a voice that's telling you it's not gonna happen. Then say to yourself as many times as you need to cast out the darkness, "Thank you. I am loved. I've got what it takes." You can do it. You will do it. You have only but to make up your mind and stay with it come rain or shine. Always give love regardless of circumstance and your circumstances are bound to change. Every single person who changed the world once was in the same position as you are, and they were no smarter or well positioned than you are. That's the truth. Many of them began with nothing. You have the keys. You only have to stay with it. Always meditate on what is of good report no matter how silly or repetitive it sounds. I have positive affirmations that I say to myself every part of the day, and they are like deposits that you make which give you the strength to remain joyful no matter what you face. That's training for the trials you're not yet in, and we've all got to do it. You will do it, and you will be victorious. Take these keys with you everywhere you go.

8. AT YOUR COMMAND

"Whatsoever you desire, when you pray believe that you have received it and you shall have it."

Jesus

The call came unexpectedly as it does for most of us. My mom was in the hospital with severe arrhythmia of the heart, which had kept up for days and it presented a significant danger. If this continued, she could have heart failure or a stroke. She signed consent forms over how things would be handled in the event of her death. The doctors had evaluated the alarm on her pacemaker and determined they must perform a risky procedure where they shock her heart back into correct rhythm. The shock could save her life, or it could end it. I could tell she's worried by the tone of her voice, and the last thing I wanted to do is add to it. Something clicked inside of me. It's an intuitive feeling. A calmness came over me. I knew what to do, but I couldn't articulate it at the time. I told her I'm on my way. In that moment our thoughts go one direction or another. The temptation in our mind is to cycle through all the possible outcomes and consider the worst. Was this for real? Could the doctors be over-reacting? There are normally dozens of scenarios to consider in a moment like that, but that's not what happened to me in that moment. I made a choice to refuse to consider the possibility that my mom would die. I would go down there to bring her joy, and I would not acknowledge the worst case scenario. My mom is a creative person. She loves to dress up in costumes, play games, and enjoy all of the childlike wonders of life. On the way over I felt a number of emotions rush through me, but all I would allow myself to think about was the laughter and smiles I would see on my mom's face and those of the nurses. I was thinking jokes I could tell her. Games we could play. I imagined her feeling great and excited. Then I got an idea to stop by the party store and pick up a hat, some goofy glasses, and a lollipop. This is just the kind of thing she would do for someone else. In a flash I grabbed the goods and was on my way into the hospital. When I walked in and found my mom being wheeled down to the intensive care unit, I got a big laugh from the nurses. They were all smiling and laughing over the goofy attire I'd put on. I looked silly but I did not care, because I was there for one reason, and that was to bring my mother joy, and that's all that mattered. She laughed and smiled all the way down to the room where they were about to shock her heart. By the time the nurses were wiring her up and preparing for the operation, the tone of the room had changed. It was tempting to look at everything that was going on and become fixated on that reality, but I refused to believe the hospital and the equipment and the nurses was our reality. I asked my mom if she wouldn't mind playing the gratitude game where each of us go back and forth to share one thing we're grateful for. It was amazing. Even the nurses couldn't help but smile and join in as an attitude of thankfulness overtook the room. They gave us a moment just before they were prepared to bring in the doctors to begin. This was it for me. I felt all of my thoughts, which I set out with the intention of bringing positive energy to my mother line up, and I approached the side of her bed. I took her hand into mine, and I asked a simple question: "do you want to be well?" She looked into my eyes and stillness came over the room. She said, "yes." And as a bolt of energy passed through my being into her hand, I responded, "then be well." I stood at the foot of the bed as the room filled with hospital staff preparing to operate. Then one of the nurses looked concerned as she studied the monitors. She quickly got on the phone speaking in a rush. Then she hung up and turned toward my mother and uttered the most shocking words of all, "Your heart has been restored. The arrhythmia is gone. We do not need to perform the procedure. You can go home." My mother had been healed in that instant and was able to get up and leave. She was stunned and so was everyone else. There's nothing to be done. She got on her clothing, and I walked her out of the hospital within about 15 minutes from that moment in complete wonder and amazement over this miraculous healing. Our bodies are capable of doing the most phenomenal things when they are given the right orders. The problem is we are often misdirecting ourselves with contradictory messages. Building up with one hand and tearing down with the other. We want healing, but when most people are sick that's all they talk about. People ask and they want to be honest. They want the sympathy, so they go on about their symptoms. Internally those messages are circulated through our electrical system. They are validated and repeated. If you want to get better, you've got to change the message of your beliefs. My mother up to that point had been validating a message that she was in great danger, but when she changed her belief and began feeling grateful, things changed. That example is one of many miraculous circumstances I've seen, and it is one of the most striking to see it take place in front of medical professionals who are convinced that shocking her heart and potentially ending her life is the only way to get her heart back on track. Now I have the utmost respect for doctors, many of whom are close friends of mine, and there is value in utilizing their abilities while you're exploring and developing confidence in your body's own ability to heal. For example, if you cut your arm, you know that your immune system has the ability to heal, but that doesn't mean you shouldn't use antibiotic ointment and bandages to further the healing process. However, there are many people I know who are going from doctor to doctor looking for solutions to problems that they hope will be resolved through a prescription when in reality they first need to change their beliefs about their own health. It sounds simple, but if you want to be healthy, start by sending your body messages that you are healthy. When you start to feel concerned about your health and those thoughts begin to overtake you, change your internal conversation, and say "thank you for my health." You can't do it too much! If you go around talking about and affirming disease that is what you will get more of. The key isn't just saying it. You've got to deny the evidence of your senses and believe you are healthy by feeling your way into that state. This is where the power comes from, because with emotional power, you are forging a new path of health with new messages. As you begin doing this, you will be amazed by the power you have to not only heal yourself, but to ignite a flame in others to recognize their own potential. Did you know that before Jesus ever performed a miracle, he always gave thanks beforehand? Was this customary? Was it a religious decision? No. Jesus understood implicitly the power of gratitude and the faith it activates in a human being to transcend their circumstances. This is why we must be ruthless with our thoughts. Never allow yourself to indulge thoughts of the worse case scenario. Drop them out of your mind. Don't go there and don't get down on yourself for having had them in the past. Instead, anytime a negative thought weaves its way back into your consciousness, just laugh at your childlike nature and then give thanks that your miracle is on its way. Giving thanks in advance is a powerful step. Visualizing the miracle as if it is already an accomplished fact and feel the joy of it realized. There's a third, fun step I've come to see work wonders in building faith. This is a step of taking imaginal baby steps in your environment like your desire has already been fulfilled. This key is exceptionally powerful for those who look at their circumstances and have difficulty believing that a miracle is possible. It supercharges your faith. Just like the case of my mother's environment at the hospital you might feel trapped and headed away from your desire. There are imaginal acts that you would do in the comfort of your own home or car to inspire your feelings to look past your circumstances and bring your inner-desire forward into manifested reality. For me, this was picking up some party supplies and bringing them down to the hospital to celebrate when from appearances, it looked like there was nothing to celebrate. If you dread getting things in the mail, try walking to the mailbox and imagine getting the best news of your life. Jump for joy and celebrate. Check your email and do a dance like the news you've been waiting for has just arrived and it's better than expected. If you're alone and hoping for a new relationship, set the table for two and genuinely feel the satisfaction of having the person of your dreams. Make the phone call and get an estimate on the kitchen remodel like you're ready to make the order. This doesn't mean you need to make the order or you need to go into debt to make it happen. These are baby steps, and they will bring about the positive feelings and thoughts, which will move mountains in your life, and miracles will come. It seems crazy, but this is actually how it works. Thoughts become things. This is something to do regularly, but never as a chore. You want to feel the excitement. As you express the faith of a child, you will be so happy, you won't even think you need it. Strangely enough, that is exactly when the manifested reality begins to move into your life. Most people are waiting for the object to feel happy, and it only leads to a cycle of discontent. If I had waited to feel joy until my mom was better, that would never have come. As you do this, you will come up with more and more ideas of imaginal baby steps to take. Remember when taking the baby steps, you are not responsible for actually bringing the desire into manifestation by force. You are aligning your thoughts and feelings in harmony with the creative powers of the Universe, so it can be brought to you. That takes the pressure off, so have fun with this key and keep using it. You will be left in wonder.

9. HIDDEN SELF-IMAGE

"The subconscious mind is ruled by suggestion, it accepts all suggestions – it does not argue with you – it fulfills your wishes."

Dr. Joseph Murphy

I grew up in a family that attended a large church, and I even went to Bible College. I had access to more spiritual understanding than most people. I had so many questions about how the mind worked and why was it that anytime I questioned anything, it was suggested if I would pray, read my Bible, and go to church with the other 12,000 other sheep, that my problems would be solved. Well I did that for years, and it just got more confusing to me. All of the Bible stories are without a doubt of great value. That was not answering my questions. I wanted to know why I was thinking what I was thinking, and why I had patterns of behavior that were at times in conflict. It wasn't until I was willing to step outside of my comfort zone of evangelical privilege that I really began to understand myself. This is not to blame my parents or the spiritual overseers who I was subject to. They were doing the very best they could with the awareness they had access to. If you have grown up in a hyper-religious setting, you too know what that feels like. Every single one of us has a conscious and a sub-conscious mind. Inside our subconscious mind, which some people refer to as the heart or soul, there is programming that has been there from your infancy. Actually, there is programming in your subconscious, which comes from your parents, grandparents, and even before that. That programming impacts every decision you make. Have you ever considered which pant leg you put on first? It's likely it's the same leg your parent puts in first as well. Most people never stop to question why they have certain habits. My mentor, Bob Proctor, who was made famous in the film "The Secret," calls these patterns of habits paradigms. We have paradigms locked in our subconscious mind, and they control every decision we make. Our conscious mind is just the tip of the iceberg. The subconscious mind holds the power to direct the ship. One illustration that clicked for me is to think of the mind like a ship. The captain is the conscious mind. He gives orders and deals with the reality right in front of him, but he can only see what he can see. The subconscious mind is the rest of the ship. It is the men running the engine. It handles the radio transmissions with the satellite and main land. The subconscious controls the inner-workings of the ship and where it goes. The subconscious is tied into your central nervous system and operates based on the beliefs, which you have held in your subconscious. It always accepts the dominant of two ideas, so that's why even if you've tried to change a certain habit through conscious willpower; your habits reverted back to the old ones. That's because you have a self-image in your subconscious. It's how you view yourself. You may have accepted ideas about yourself, which are completely false. You may have accepted that you're a failure or not qualified to pursue your dreams, because of what your parents told you. It could be total nonsense! Yet, if you believed it long enough, then it has become your dominant belief, and your subconscious has faithfully executed those orders like the men in the engine room of a steamship responding to the captain. It should be noted that some of the programming passed down to us from our parents is not harmful. "Don't touch the stove! That will burn you!" "Don't step out into the street, you'll get run over!" "Don't eat that rat poison! It will kill you!" Those habits are healthy. Unfortunately, they have also passed down habits and beliefs which limit you based on fears or insecurities your parents and grandparents held in their mind.

"Our self-image and our habits tend to go together. Change one and you will automatically change the other."

Dr. Maxwell Maltz

The awesome part of this realization is that your self-image creates your reality, and you can change this self-image. In Dr. Maxwell Maltz's book, he explains that as a plastic surgeon people would come to him asking for a face-lift or nose job, and he discovered their real problem was the self-image they were holding in their mind. Once they changed their self-image and began to see themselves as they desired, something marvelous happened. They not only were much happier, they began to see that others saw them differently, and their whole life began to change. There is a false perception that certain people are better than others. The truth is inferiority and superiority are opposite sides of the same coin. We've all been blessed with the same amount of potential as the most high profile people in the world. Many people have a low estimate of themselves, and it doesn't have to be that way. The problem is that we are conditioned to look outside ourselves for the solution to our problems. Trying to change your life by changing something outside is like trying to change the reflection in your mirror without changing your physical appearance. You're trying in vain. If you want to discover the kind of self-image you have, it's not hard to find out. All you've got to do is look at the results you're getting in your life. Look at your relationships, your income, your work, and your habits. Waiting for change to happen is to hope in vain. You've got to change your self-image if you want your life to turn out the way you like. How do you begin to do that? Should you see a counselor? Should you increase your attendance at church? Those are all conditions. They are outer expressions of an inner belief about yourself. If you want to change your life, you must look within. Neville Goddard, who was one of the first people in the 20th century to make this understanding available in America, pointed out brilliantly that you should never try to change anyone else's opinion of you. They will only express in the open what you have whispered to them in secret. The view that you are holding about yourself in your subconscious will always be expressed in the screen of space. Our subconscious mind is a marvelous faculty. It is connected to what I think of as the central nervous system of the entire Universe. God's entire creation is tapped into and connected with our subconscious mind. People don't seem to have a difficult time believing that fearful beliefs create fearful circumstances, especially if you're someone who was programmed in the church. Job of Biblical fame cried, "That which I have greatly feared has come upon me." He feared something and it came about. You create your own reality. That is a power you've been given. Are you holding fears in your mind? Dr. Viktor Frankl wrote about fears in his chilling testimony of his survival of the Holocaust, "A Man's Search For Meaning." A fear brings about that which it fears. At Auschwitz, Victor saw that when a man had given up on himself, death was imminent. If one of his fellow prisoners refused to get up out of the bed in the morning, and they chose to stay in the sewage of their hut, rather than work in the frigid cold out of hope that they might survive, it was often only a short time before he perished from illness. If however a man had a hope or an image in their mind of a life that awaited them, it gave them the necessary power to continue on much longer. For Dr. Viktor Frankl this lead to his rare and miraculous survival, where 27 out of 28 other men around him disintegrated. A self-image in a case like the Holocaust literally means the difference between life and death. However, Viktor also discovered that if a person were to associate meaning to their suffering and overcome the neurosis by doing the opposite of what they were afraid to do, usually the fear dissipated in patients he worked with following the Holocaust. Bob Proctor, who is a world renowned author and speaker, refers to this as the terror barrier. When we do the thing we are afraid to do, the fear will subside. When you think of recreating your self-image, you might have fears that crop up. What if I can't? What if I fail? What if it doesn't happen for me? Is this selfish? What will others think of me? You don't need to concern yourself with that. You can be of most help to others when you appreciate yourself. When you don't think well of yourself, you're naturally going to not think well of others. We naturally project on others what we think of ourselves. It's time to begin to recreate our self-image. In order to do that, we're going to have to allow ourselves to dream, always keeping in mind the golden rule, "doing unto others as we would have them do unto us." We should never engage in a view of ourselves that would be of harm to others, because anything we do to them will always come back around to us. As long as we understand that, there should be no limitation placed on how big your dreams are. It was some of the most unreasonable men who changed the course of history. The Wright Brothers were unreasonable, and they were determined to fly when nobody else believed it. Now we all benefit from it. Decide who you are right now in your mind. Imagine it. See it. Feel it. Right now begin to see yourself as that person. Take the lid off. Let your mind soar. It doesn't matter how old you are. Whether you are 18 or 80, it's time to dream. Anytime a doubt comes to your mind, cast it aside as a sin. Let your mind take flight. Imagine yourself doing the things you desire to do in the first person. Engage all of your senses. Smell the air. Touch the objects you would touch. Hear the reactions of friends congratulating you on your success. For anyone who has built up resistance on this topic seeing it as indulgent, remember that Proverbs makes it very clear "Without a vision, people perish." Most often people think this is someone else's vision for them… It's your vision! You've got to have a vision, and the key to learning is repetition. In "Psycho-Cybernetics," Dr. Maxwell Maltz asserts that it takes 21 days to form a new habit in your mind. I've seen this to be the case in my own life and watched tremendous results come to pass often effortlessly when I employed a new-self image. I'd suggest that for the next 21 days, you set aside a minimum of 15-20 minutes each day to close out the world around you. Possibly first thing in the morning before the events of the day have started up, visualize yourself being the person you desire to be. After you're done visualizing, create a written description of your life in the present tense. Always begin "I'm so happy and grateful now that..." Define your life as you'd like it to be. You will notice differences between your description and your life as it is now. When you go back to your life, don't try to force it to happen. That will create more resistance. You must practice detachment from your circumstances. Do not grow discouraged that your conditions do not line up to your vision. This will happen automatically. Accept your present circumstances as only your present reality, because they are only a shadow of past decisions. These circumstances and your old behaviors will fade away as you form a new self-image through repetition of daily visualization. Continue to visualize yourself each day. If you have a health condition, financial struggles, or relationship issues, it is of utmost importance that you move your attention and your feelings to the state of the wish fulfilled. You can begin to feel healthy, and even if you don't see those results in your life, do not worry. Worry does nothing for you or anyone else. Keep your vision of yourself to yourself! Do not brag about it, nor should you complain about your present circumstances to others. All that does is reaffirm those conditions to yourself and to others. It is very foolish to complain to others about your problems, because it strengthens the problems by planting seeds in the minds of others. This is why Jesus said "pray without ceasing." He spoke for all people, not only the hyper-religious. This is the essence of living the state of our self-image and feeling it to be true every moment of every day, regardless of whether we have any evidence of it whatsoever with our senses. I started with 30 minutes a day of visualizing, and very often the feelings of those imaginings became so powerful and so real, they have lifted my spirit to such a state of joy I felt I didn't even need the manifestation. This is the essence of joy. When we feel a visualization to be true so much where we don't even need it, most often it is at that point where the manifestation becomes inevitable. Yes, when that feeling overcomes me, it is not long before I see an immediate change of my conditions. I don't know how it happens, but it does work. I began visualizing once a day, and now I have increased to 3x a day. This results in a residual effect that is so strong, regardless of what is happening throughout my day. The joy of my vision continues to penetrate those circumstances and those around me naturally become part of my imaginal drama. I am constantly full of joy and able to look for ways to help others. When we feel low and depleted, we can hardly help ourselves much less help others.

In his book, Dr. Maltz tells of a chess player who was going up against the top chess player in the world. He knew he was the underdog and scarcely stood a chance to win if he went about his preparation the usual way. He decided to do something different. He quit drinking, smoking, and even quite playing chess for the three months leading up to the match. Instead, he set aside time each day to visualize himself playing the titan of a chess player and winning. Each day, he practiced only in his mind, and every time he came to a successful outcome. Three months later, the underdog beat the reigning world champion, and the world of chess stood in shock. Reporters asked what his secret was. When he told them he played no chess to get ready and only visualized his victory, they were amazed. Dr. Maltz asserted that although the exact strategies his opponent used were not the ones he used in the match, his subconscious mind was inclined toward victory, and since the subconscious is wired into the entire universal knowledge of our Creator, it wisely moved his consciousness to make the right moves to win. The odds were against him, and yet it did not matter. He was victorious because he created a self-image that was clear. He felt himself into the state of victory. He had the winning feeling. He persisted in that feeling until it became his dominating belief and victory belonged to him. Many athletes and businessmen can relate to what Dr. Maltz refers to as the winning feeling. When you have it, you know you're going to succeed. When you're first starting out on this journey and you've perhaps formed a strong paradigm of negative beliefs and habits about yourself, it can be difficult to visualize and feel yourself into a state of your desired life. If this happens, you have a tool that can help you move your mind in a positive direction like a pair of crutches until you learn to walk. Get out your journal and make a list of memories in your life where you felt good about yourself or successful in a certain activity. These can be very small things like learning to ride a bike or tying your shoe, or they could be very big things like graduating from school, completing a race, or anything else that makes you feel good about yourself. Dr. Maltz says these experiences can be remembered time and again to bring us back to that winning feeling. You can dwell on one of these memories and it will develop in you the confidence to believe you are capable being what you desire to be. Use them as a springboard when you start your visualization if you are experiencing negative feelings. For me a memory that works is beating the game Mario Bros. when I was five years old and calling my dad to tell him. I was so excited about this I couldn't wait to tell my dad of my success. I had played the game over and over, failing every time. That game was a beast for me. Achieving victory was like winning the Olympics, and I wanted to share that victory with my dad. I have gone back to that memory many times, and it has brought me tremendous joy, and much more. It has enabled me the forward momentum in my mind to imagine and believe that I can achieve my dreams. You can too! You've got everything you need within you! You've got the power! Start with some positive memories to keep in your tool belt you can draw on, then let your mind soar each day, imagining your life as you'd like it to be. If you can hold it in your mind, you can hold it in your hand. Be patient with yourself as you build your new self-image. At a time when you least expect it, your life will magically re-shape itself in perfect harmony with the dream you're holding in your mind. Now let your mind take flight and watch as your wonderful imagination creates your reality!

10. LIVING THE DREAM

When I was fourteen years old, my parents were so busy getting ready for our Christmas vacation, they completely forgot my birthday. That day I was so excited, I felt like I might burst. I kept my lips zipped. I was sure they were planning a surprise party for me. All day long, I perceived every look as if they were keeping a secret for when we arrived at our condo in Breckenridge, Colorado. When we went inside, no surprise party awaited me, just an empty condo. I kept my hopes high, maybe they were waiting to surprise me when I got in bed, so I didn't say anything. I waited until everyone else fell asleep, and then it hit me. They forgot my birthday. I gently scuttled into my parents bedroom and shook my mom, "Hey mom, did you know it was my birthday today?" They both sat up in bed, wide eyed in shock like the parents in Home Alone. I was melancholy for months after that. Out of five kids in my family, why is it that they could remember everyone else's birthday but not mine? Was there something wrong with me? Did I need to be somebody else? Well, six months later on June 26 my parents surprised me with a big surprise party and bought me a video camera, mountain bike, and a TV. They had never done this for any of the kids. It turned out that my greatest disappointment as a child resulted in my greatest advantage. At last, I had the tool I needed to make the films I desperately craved to make.

That situation was most certainly a blessing in disguise. I had imagined having a video camera for a long time, and it came when I was least expecting it. Your conscious mind expects something to come a certain way, and you are disappointed when it doesn't, like I was on my birthday. However, someone much more capable has better plans for you. This is why it's so important to determine what you want, not how it will come. You must persist in the feeling of the wish fulfilled, and you may find that your greatest disappointment will turn out to be your greatest victory. Had my parents remembered my blessed birthday, they probably never would have sprung for a video camera. Back then, a high-8 digital video camera with an LCD screen cost a pretty penny for a pastor supporting five kids in a mobile home. Someone above was looking out for me, who knew that forgetting my birthday and all the humiliation that followed with my brother and sister poking fun at me, was actually the best thing for me to realize what I really wanted. There's a greater lesson in store than even our little desires. Over the years, this experience has taught me that satisfying our wants will never bring us total fulfillment. We will always be in want. In fact, those wants our conscious mind craves in part are really limited to what we can see, and the truth is, we are really part of all that is in the Universe already. We are connected to every other person out there. Quantum physics states we are made up of subatomic particles, which are made up of energy. Everything is made out of energy, and that is why the competitive mindset is really ignorance at its worst.

"What you recognize in others,
you recognize in yourself."

Neville Goddard

When you see others behaving in a way that displeases you like my parents did on my birthday, or perhaps when you see employers or politicians make decisions that anger you, it's easy to succumb to an attitude of frustration and hate. These negative feelings keep you from achieving success in your mind and in your circumstances. The anger inside can make you in the image of that very negative quality. You cannot have a negative attitude toward others and achieve any lasting success. To paraphrase Buddha, "You inevitably burn yourself when you hold a hot coal intending to throw it at others."

Understanding that we are one with all that is out there is the highest spiritual achievement our minds can rise to. If you doubt that, consider the practical matter of what happens to your energy when you die.

Does it not return to the energy that is connected with everything else in the Universe? Why then would you invest a single moment of the limited time you have on this earth to pretend that little old you is the only one that is separate from everyone else. Yes, there are people who commit terrible crimes in this world, but they do so out of ignorance, and to give energy to them is to perpetuate that quality by planting those seeds within yourself and others. Why then would you invest your energy in thinking about them and talking about them?

If our world could fully grasp this concept, we would advance infinitely in harmony as a society. This is possible, and it's not only possible, it's my conviction that it is inevitable. Many people give lip service to the idea that God is love and He is omnipresent. In the same conversation, they will rail on this religion or that politician. If God is in all and through all, then He is in those people as well and to condemn them is to condemn God and also to condemn yourself. There is no separation. There is no us against them. When you fully accept that fact, you will begin to experience peace, and you will see the interconnectedness of everything in your life.

For many years, I pretended to be separate from others, and I started to see a pattern that when I looked or acted negatively toward someone, it would come back around from somewhere else in my life like a boomerang. When I began to appreciate that we are all connected, it became about the difference I could make in the lives of others. When we look out for others, we are naturally looked out for. This happens automatically. Do not look out for others with the expectation that you will get something in return. Give without expectation. This is where there is the greatest joy. That's real giving, and when we do, inevitably we receive from people who also give cheerfully. Can you see why that makes sense? When you find it difficult to give, you will assume it's difficult for people to give to you. If you assume it's easy to give, you will assume it's easy to receive. You will be proven right. It's a slight shift, but watch what happens as you do it. It's astonishing!

Next time you have to tip that waiter or give to that charity, do so cheerfully. Every time! If nothing else proves to you things are connected, you will see that instantly. This is one of the most wondrous realizations. Live in joyous expectancy of the best and the best will come to you. Look every day for the difference you can make in the lives of others. If you deal with depression or sadness about your goals not taking place, I'm going to give you a secret as old as the ages. Whatever you want to make happen in your life, make that happen in someone else's life. Find someone else who is depressed and cheer them up. If you need money, find a way to give. If you are looking for opportunities, connect others with opportunities. Watch how this secret makes things change for you, daily. Remember not to expect anything back from the people you gave to! That is a cardinal sin. It will come back to you in a way you least expect it, but more importantly, the joy you will experience from helping others will be priceless. The joy will multiply endlessly. That is the purpose of life. Not the accumulation of possessions or riches. This is the greatest folly, because you can't take that with you. Your joy remains with you as you pass on, so in all your getting receive this wisdom. As you do this, everything else will be added unto you for a satisfied and success filled life. I want to thank you for embarking on this journey, and I'm excited for you to change your life as you use your imagination to create the reality of your dreams. You've got what it takes!

FURTHER READING

The Power of Awareness
Neville Goddard

As a Man Thinketh
James Allen

Psycho-Cybernetics
Maxwell Maltz

The Magic of Believing
Claude M. Bristol

Working with the Law
Raymond Holliwell

Lead the Field
Earl Nightingale

The Art of Living
Bob Proctor

The Alchemist
Paulo Coelho

The Power of Your Subconscious Mind
Dr. Joseph Murphy

The Power
Rhonda Byrne

Happy Pocket Full of Money
David Cameron Gikandi

The Science of Getting Rich
Wallace D. Wattles

The Greatest Salesman in the World
Og Mandino

Think and Grow Rich
Napoleon Hill

Made in the USA
Middletown, DE
22 April 2019